Int | AR

Interventions | Adaptive Reuse

Editors In Chief:
Markus Berger
Liliane Wong

Graphic Design Editor:
Ernesto Aparicio

Int|AR is an annual publication by the editors in chief: Markus Berger + Liliane Wong, and the Department of Interior Architecture, Rhode Island School of Design.

Layout + Design Coordination_Cara Buzzell, Sungkyu Yang
Editorial + Communications Assistant_Toban Shadlyn
Cover Design_Ernesto Aparicio, Cara Buzzell
Cover Photo_Browning Cottage, Matunuck, RI_Aerial Photograph by John Supancic
Inner Cover Photos_Markus Berger, Jeremy Wolin
Support Team_Iris Kuo
Copyediting_Amy Doyle, Clara Halston, Jeremy Wolin
Printed by SYL, Barcelona
Distributed by Birkauser Verlag GmbH, Basel P.O. Box 44, 4009 Basel, Switzerland,
Part of Walter de Gruyter GmbH, Berlin/Boston

Int|AR Journal welcomes responses to articles in this issue and submissions of essays or projects for publication in future issues. All submitted materials are subject to editorial review. Please address feedback, inquiries, and other material to the Editors, Int|AR Journal, Department of Interior Architecture, Rhode Island School of Design, Two College Street, Providence, RI 02903 www.intar-journal.edu, email: INTARjournal@risd.edu

CONTENTS

EDITORIAL

PROJECTING CHANGE

FROM NEWPORT TO SÃO PAOLO BY WAY OF VENICE

by LILIANE WONG

5th century B.C. Greek philosopher Empedocles posited a world composed of a combination of fire, earth, air, and water. Half a century later, Plato, in his dialogue *Timaeus*, termed these as elements and associated them with forms now referred to as the Platonic solids. Fire was associated with the tetrahedron, earth with the cube, air with the octahedron, and water with the twenty-sided icosahedron. Ostensibly, these volumetric associations related to identifying traits of each element; the sharp points of the tetrahedron conjuring the heat of fire, the cloddish quality of the cube to clumps of earth and the smoothness of the many-sided icosahedron to spherical drops of water. From sustenance to survival, inspiration, memory and power, the many aspects of and about water justify its designation as the Platonic solid with the greatest number of faces.

In Volume 08, our contributing authors corroborate Plato's multifaceted depiction and provide a complex picture of this element as a catalyst for design and adaptation. Through adaptive reuse, the temporal nature of infrastructure/structures of and about water is revealed as they are brought forward in time with renewed purpose, or, in the case of Erbil, Iraq, returned in time to resuscitate an important socio-cultural function. Memory and memorial of water-related events past reveal distant histories of the United States through the properties of water in its many states and its comingling with other substances. Outside the U.S., water is portrayed as a catalyst for urban development in Spain, agro-tourism for Albania and a trigger for environmental policy in Brazil. The life within the waters, too, inspire new perspectives; reinterpreted oyster habitats in the Chesapeake Bay and an unanticipated appropriation of space for today's coterie of *flâneurs* in the koi filled waters of Bangkok.

In this post-Paris Agreement era, many of our authors focus on water's role in climate change. They remind us of the force of nature and the strength of water as elements to be contended with in the environment. In recognition that this is not a novel problem, recollections of water management in history not only resurrect exemplary water strategies — from the *chinampas* of Mexico to hydrographic basins in the American West - but also remind us that design has served and can continue to serve as a catalyst for political ideology. On the other hand, acknowledging the immensity of water as power, one author ponders a unique approach for the future in which we accept mortality and design for failure.

Our authors and their representation of the many faces of water in this issue of *Int|AR* speak to a changing world in which water plays a pivotal role. In the Department of Interior Architecture at RISD, where the focus is on the practice of adaptive reuse, we also look to understanding the changing face of reusing existing structures at the water's edge. Thanks to the generosity of the van Beuren Charitable Foundation and the Newport Restoration Foundation, graduate students of our post-professional Master of Arts (MA) in Adaptive Reuse program are focusing this spring on the changing face of heritage in Newport, RI. In this 378-year old city on the water are embodied many issues of American historic buildings and cities today, including the impact of sea level rise. With 39% of the U.S. population living on the water's edge, this is of particular relevance at Easton's Point, a 17th century settlement along the western shoreline. While this area has historically experienced extreme storms, high tides and storm surge, the National Oceanic and Atmospheric Administration (NOAA) model adopted in 2016 by the RI Coastal Resources Management Council predicts 1 foot of sea level rise by 2035. For this historic community, built on grade, the possibility of inundation is far from remote.

This year's cohort of MA graduate students will undertake to 'project change', literally and figuratively, onto Easton's Point. Co-taught by Markus Berger,

Michael Grugl and me, the project addresses Bridge Street in the Point Neighborhood and extends the work begun in the *Keeping 74 Bridge Street Above Water* project of our co-sponsor, Newport Restoration Foundation (NRF). Where NRF's project focused on immediate and tangible solutions for a single historic house combatting sea level rise in the next decade, the RISD project, *Projecting Change*, instead focuses on raising public awareness of the effects of sea level rise on cultural heritage.

The students are conducting their investigations on issues of preservation in historic neighborhoods seriously threatened by rising sea water levels through the use of new data acquisition technology, together with state of the art visualization and processing technology such as Augmented Reality (AR) and Virtual Reality (VR). The objective in using these digital tools with virtual building models is to engage a general public, at times skeptical and inured to the dangers of climate change for waterfront heritage. The visualization of these objectives through Mixed Reality tools will allow for the creation of an immersive and interactive built environment that enables the public to 'see,' in situ, the physical effects of rising sea levels on a threatened area of Easton's Point. Through a mobile device, the citizen will experience a neighborhood transformed in the future through proposed, virtual design interventions.

Embracing the impermanence enabled by such technology, the studio endeavors to intervene on the heritage of Newport, without encroaching upon its authenticity. Through a projection of temporary imagery directly onto buildings, this project aims to pose questions of the not-too-distant future of such heritage. One can 'try on' an inundated Bridge Street in 2035 with the luxury of retreating to the Bridge Street of today. For a heritage-laden Newport threatened by sea level rise, realization, and perhaps even a call to action, may eventually come with exposure to small glimpses of the future. These glimpses will perhaps convince the public that design interventions to heritage are no longer simply part of a privileged conversation but, rather, a new and urgent discussion that will push the boundaries of preservation and adaptive reuse. On May 26, we will host an event on Bridge Street in which Google Cardboard viewers and mixed reality markers will offer five glimpses into the possible future of this historic community. The projects – Walking on Water, Grey-Green-Blue, Memory Trace, Up-Struct and The Game – provide views of Bridge Street in a future in which water is catalyst. They offer new interpretations of what it means to "protect, accommodate, retreat." We offer the same augmented reality opportunity for our readers, with directions on the following page.

My colleagues and I had the opportunity to present the work of this studio in New Orleans, Louisiana, at the 3D Digital Documentation conference of the U.S. Dept. of the Interior. In this vibrant city, more than a decade after devastation by water, we spoke with members of the architectural firm of Waggoner and Ball who spearheaded the multi-layered efforts for "living with water," post-Katrina. While they have worked tirelessly since 2005, there is only now talk of the implementation of the schemes arising from their work. This inertia is evident in Governor John Bel Edwards' April 19th official declaration of a state of emergency for Louisiana's coastal land loss, "a move he hopes will expedite a host of restoration projects mired in federal permitting. In his declaration, the governor said that "The Louisiana coast is in a state of crisis that demands immediate and urgent action to avert further damage to one of our most vital resources." While many now engage in designing for the effects of water, the implications of the long time efforts of Waggoner and Ball speak to the need for not only design but collaboration, economic initiatives, community engagement, education and, most of all, endurance.

Late one afternoon we drove away from New Orleans through inundated landscapes of semi-submerged trees to Venice, marked simply by a sign that read, "you have reached the southernmost point in Louisiana." The last community down the Mississippi River that is accessible by car, Venice (population of 200+ inhabitants) was entirely destroyed by Katrina but has since rebuilt itself as a floating community on buoyant foundations as well as buildings elevated high up above the water's reach. We delighted in the visible evidence of resilience, borne of water as catalyst.

Today, in a world shifting beneath our feet, the need for positive adaptation is not exclusive. Through Int|AR — the RISD studio and this publication on adaptive reuse — we embrace these challenges through projecting our hopes for change.

Providence
Spring 2017

ENDNOTES:

1 http://oceanservice.noaa.gov/facts/population.html

2 Louisiana's Governor Declares State Of Emergency Over Disappearing Coastline," National Public Radio, April 20, 2017

2017

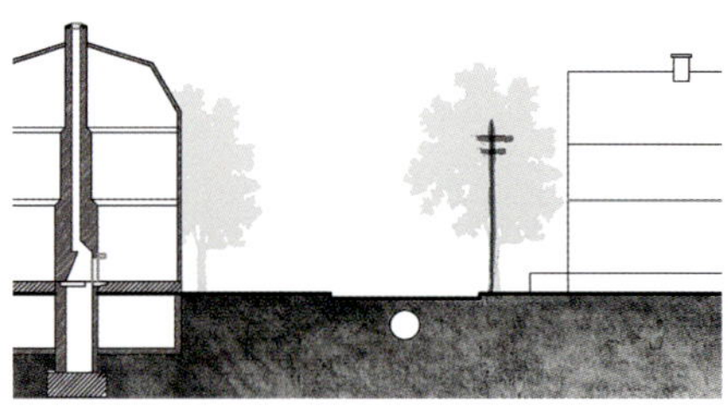

2025

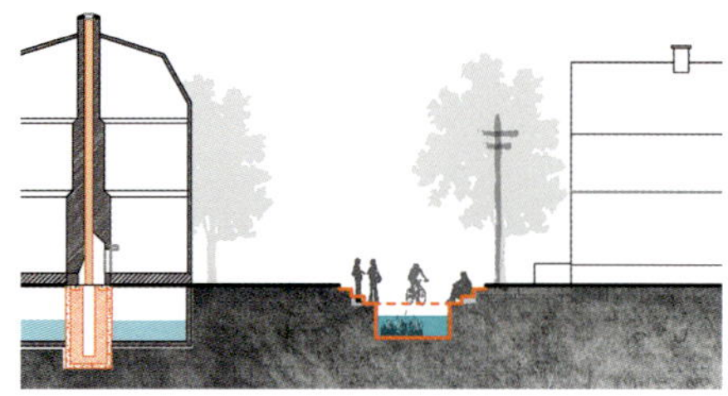

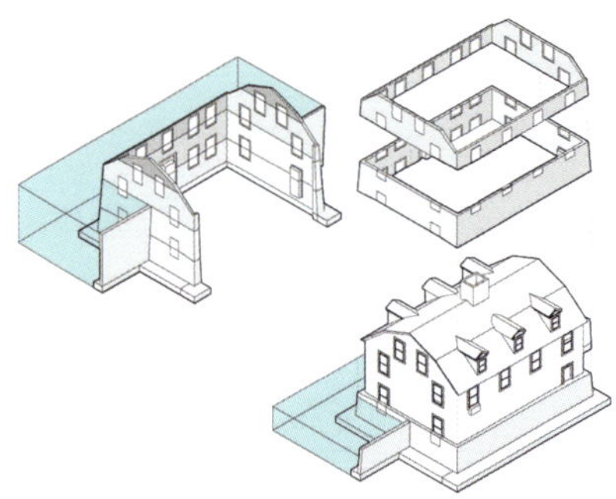

The five projects, herein, of the RISD Master of Arts in Adaptive Reuse students offer uniquely different views for an historic community threatened by sea level rise in the next 75 years. These projects were shared with the Newport community in an augmented reality event in May 2017. The students have created virtual and augmented reality experiences for this edition of the Int|AR Journal on Water as Catalyst. To learn more about the project 'Projecting Change' and to access and activate this experience on your mobile device, please go to http://www.vbcf-risd.com

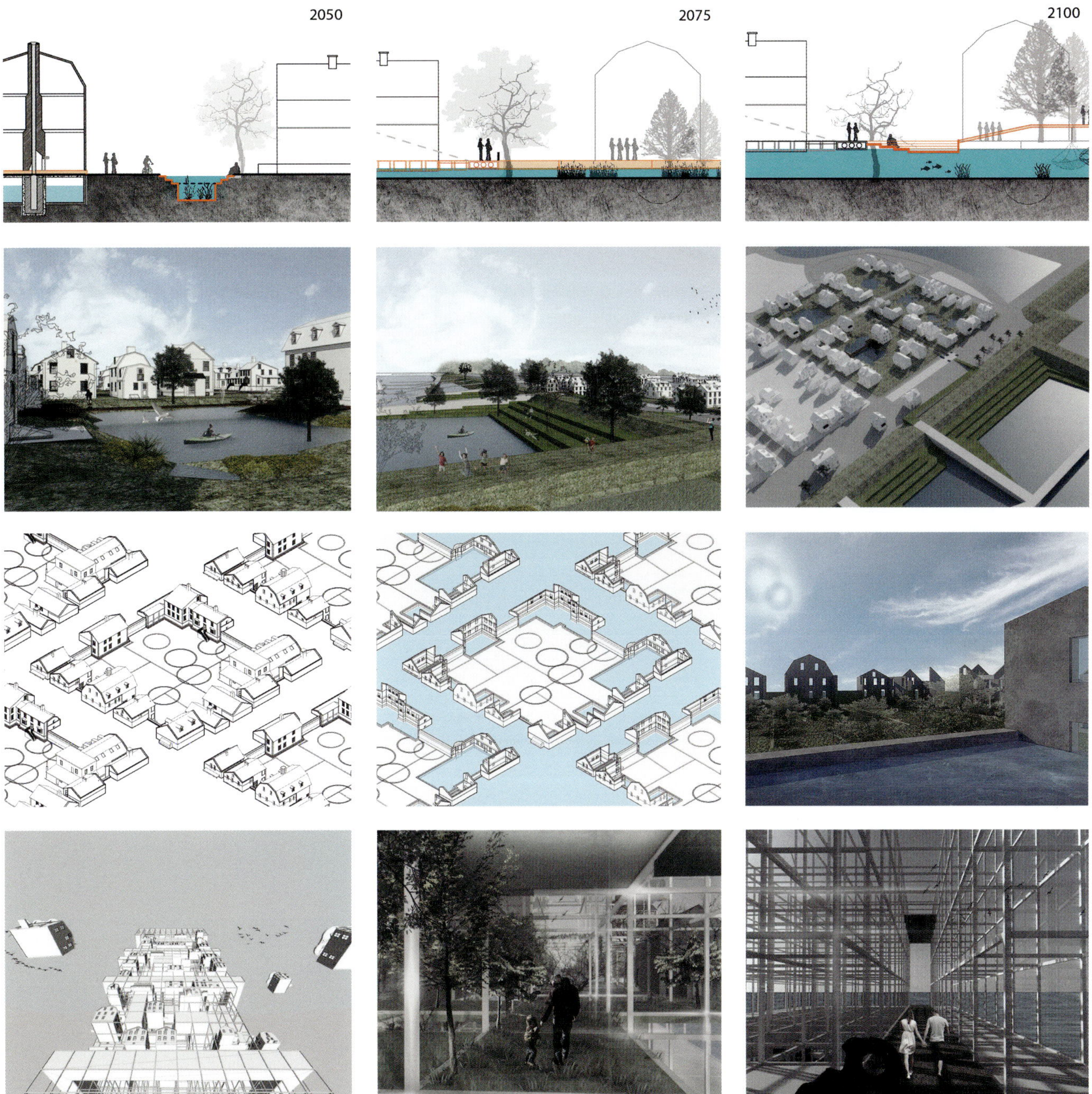

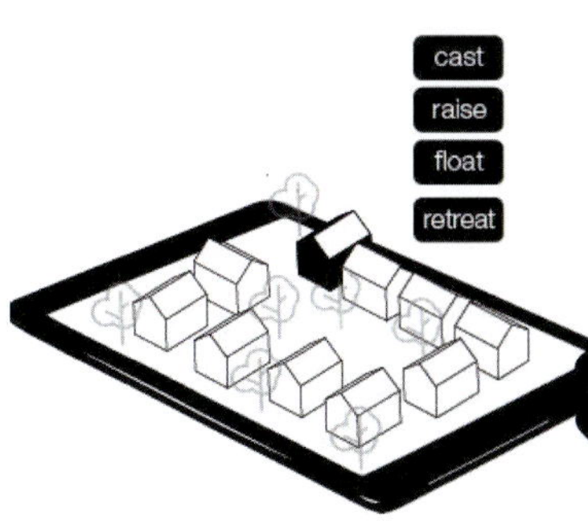

Project Change Proposals: (from top to bottom)
Walking on Water, Grey-Green-Blue, Memory Trace, Up-Struct, The Game

McMillan Slow Sand Filtration Site
Washington, DC

BREATHE, LOOK, STAND UP

THE SECOND LIFE OF WATER INFRASTRUCTURE

by LINDSAY WINSTEAD

Throughout history, access to water dictated the location of civilizations. Water transport became essential as humankind transformed from a nomadic to a sedentary culture. The development from simplistic drainage channels to complex plumbing networks allowed water to be transported from place to place, as systems deployed to collect, distribute and filter a resource vital to the growth of civilizations.

Early civilizations relied on a close proximity to a fresh water source, with the first known civilization situated between the Tigris and Euphrates Rivers. With subsequent settlements established miles from a water source, the need for water supply to these outer regions triggered infrastructure development. Although commonly accredited to the Romans, water transport infrastructure can be traced back to before the 7th century BC, when irrigation was the main purpose. The first substantial aqueduct, Aqua Appida, was erected in 312 BC and spanned a distance of 16km to service the city of Rome. While water infrastructure has evolved in scope, scale and complexity, the supply of water remains a logistical challenge. Today this resource travels many miles through networks often hidden from the public eye.

The need for sanitation is in tandem with the development of water supply infrastructure. The massive westward expansion initiated by the Industrial Revolution in the United States resulted in the exponential growth of cities and ensuing overpopulation. This high-density urban living caused outbreaks of diseases that often transferred through water. The spread of diseases such as typhoid and cholera resulted in public health concerns during the 19th century. These epidemics were addressed, in part, through the construction of sewer systems that helped to separate wastewater from clean water. Further developments in sanitation were implemented through the use of chemical treatment as well as sedimentation systems, which filtered water before use. These advanced interconnected systems have permitted a more hygienic expansion of urban life.

Defined as a "set of interconnected structural elements that provide framework supporting an entire development," water's infrastructure has become a key feature in maintenance and day-to-day operations of a city. The continuous expansion of the water supply and the development of water treatment methods demand a constant evolution in the infrastructure. What of obsolescent infrastructure?

Since water sustains itself without the need for air or light, and conforms to any shape, the infrastructure needed for water's containment is simple and many of the spaces designed for its distribution are now underground. As such, the infrastructure that supplies water constitutes a specific typology that does not necessitate human presence. How can one adapt a building type not intended for human habitation, without requisite ventilation, light, or consideration of human proportions? A second life for such infrastructure must incorporate these three requirements.

Separated by distance both physical and cultural, two projects — the DC Exchange in the US and Public Folly in China have in common the conversion of water's infrastructure that incorporates the human elements of ventilation, light, and proportion.

Case Study 1: DC Exchange

Site: *McMillan Slow Sand Filtration Site*
Location: *NW Washington DC, United States*
Size: *25 acres*
Operation: *1905 - 1986*
Proposed Rehabilitation: *2014*
Original Architect: *Army Corp of Engineers*
Proposed Design: *Lindsay Winstead*
Original Use: *Slow Sand Water Filtration center*
Rehabilitation Use: *Community Center, Marketplace, Performance space*

The McMillan Slow Sand Filtration site in Washington, DC, filtered water from the Potomac River, transported by the Washington Aqueduct, from 1905 to 1986. Revolutionary at the time, this chemical free filtration of water through two feet of sand eliminated the typhoid epidemic in Washington, DC. This site was an engineering wonder, constructed by the Army Corps of Engineers

At the McMillan Slow Sand Filtration site, the barrel-vaulted ceilings culminate in a 3-foot diameter manhole

while Frederic Law Olmstead Jr. designed its landscape. The area under the site is divided into 20 one-acre subterranean barrel-vaulted cells and two service courts that house 20 sand bins, 4 regulator houses, and 12 sanitary sand washers.

Although this filtration site is expansive, its original purpose and even existence are unknown to most DC inhabitants. One would think that its structural brilliance and architectural splendor would gain renowned recognition, at least locally and throughout architectural circles. Unfortunately, this is not the case. Its purpose was forgotten once its function became obsolete in 1986 and a more rapid sand filtration site was constructed adjacent to the existing reservoir. Because of this, there is a divide between the neighborhoods surrounding the McMillan Site, and its closure has only exacerbated conflict. The dispute between redevelopment and reuse has been in question for years. Thus, the proposed rehabilitation of the McMillan site into the DC Exchange, a marketplace—a place for expansive gatherings, spontaneous encounters, and personal exchange—would not only activate an obsolete structure but would at the same time strengthen public interaction and create a sense of community.

Case Study 2: Public Folly

Site: *People's Liberation Army No. 1102*
Location: *Shenyang, China*
Size: *20 sq meters*
Operation: *1959–1961*
Rehabilitation: *2012*
Original Architect: *Communist Party of China*
Rehabilitation Architect: *META-Project*
Original Use: *Water tower*
Rehabilitation Use: *Exhibition space, Mini Theatre, Viewing deck*

A water tower was constructed in 1959 for industrial production and was located within a dilapidated military campus called the People's Liberation Army No.1102. Founded during the Great Leap Forward, a social and economic campaign led by the Communist Party of China under Mao Zedong, this military factory helped transform China into a socialist society through rapid industrialization. Marked as one of the most significant industrial production regions of China, the Tiexi District water tower was used to supply water for the heavy production needs of factory No. 1102. Even after its disuse, this water tower was well preserved with the hopes of future integration. This vision was realized in 2012 by META-Project, a research and design based firm, which converted this water tower into what is now the Public Folly. While preserving the memory of China's industrial past, META-Project was commissioned by the Chinese real estate firm Vanke to reactivate this

Light box interventions, Public Folly

historically rich site. Without deconstructing the original water tower, the Public Folly adds a new chapter to the tower's history. Through the insertion of two end-to-end funnels, a new interior skin echoes the main installation space. Within its shell, the Public Folly provides space for community activity and performances, while its exterior brightens up the surrounding landscape. META-Project's reuse of this water tower has reactivated its role and involvement in the community.

Breathe In: Air

Similar to water, the flow of air takes the path of least resistance. While prevalent outside, air has difficulty entering contained areas. The circulation of air into a structure designed for water is a feat in itself because of the thickness of walls and its below-grade existence. Water can flow without the presence of oxygen, but humans need a consistent exchange of air within a space. Thus, interventions must take place for air to circulate throughout obsolete infrastructure.

The integration of air circulation within the DC Exchange references the site's original sand washing and replacement cycle and mimics the subterranean distribution network. Below the sand floor of the McMillan cells is a network of water pipes that distributed naturally filtered water for potable use. Within the service court, sand collectors existed for the storage of sand after being cleaned within the industrial washers. Originally the washed sand was kept in these bins and then re-distributed through hoses that pumped the sand back into each cell through above grade manholes or the service ramp. Similar to this process, the DC Exchange repurposes these industrial towers to house new air-handling units. Due to the sand collectors' elevation and the site's lack of built structures, the towers can pull in clean air for supply and return circulated air. Once air is collected it is then transported through ducts that run below ground, mimicking the obsolete water pipes, and enters the cell through floor vents. Return ducting brings circulated air back to the sand bin to either be rejected or re-circulated into the cell through an energy recovery unit. This two-fold ventilation system makes use of the cell's below-grade properties by repelling heat into the ground in the summer and maintaining heat within the ducts during the winter. The DC Exchange's ventilation system preserves the site's integrity through the utilization of its historic structures. Although complex, this method of adaptation creates a similarity between McMillan's past and proposed purpose.

As the systems developed for air circulation have been refined for efficiency and design, a portion of these systems always requires exposure to natural airflow. This basic ventilation approach is the method used in META-Project's Public Folly. Due to the extreme height of the water tower, an abundance of naturally circulating air exists around the site. The original water tower already possesses a number of small voids within its cylindrical form, making the integration of air simple. The existing rectangular openings act as air intake and release ducts, allowing cool air to enter at the bottom and warm air to rise and exit at the top. With the removal of the existing door, a funnel-like steel entrance was added at the base of the water tower, creating an open-air pavilion where air circulates directly from the exterior to the interior. Public Folly's ventilation strategy is simple and causes minimal disruption to the tower's original form.

Look: Light

Containment of water is the main purpose for its infrastructure of impregnable walls, constructed in various materials and volumes. This results in a completely enclosed environment, often times located below grade with little to no access to light. Amidst this darkness, the flow of water is unaffected. However, the integration of light is required for human occupancy.

Two methods are used for the integration of light into the subterranean DC Exchange: natural light, both direct and reflected, and electrical light. Each cavernous cell within the McMillan Slow Sand Filtration site is constructed around a 14 x 14 foot column grid, whose barrel-vaulted ceilings culminate in a 3-foot diameter manhole. The regular distribution of the structural grid below ground is mimicked by the circular manholes at its surface. Initially these manholes were used to pump freshly cleaned sand back into the 20 filtration cells. The DC Exchange's approach to lighting requires the removal of the existing manhole covers to bring natural light into the cell below. On the surface, each manhole will be fitted with high performance glass and the shaft's opening will be wrapped in a Mylar treatment to help reflect surface light into the cell. Once light enters the marketplace below, quilted aluminum storage shelves will not only help with insulation, but also with distruibuting the light horizontally. These shelves are designed with a bowed outer face to increase the reflections of sunlight. The angle distributes light at varying degrees depending on where the light rays hit the shelves' surface. In addition, supplemental electricity is needed to illuminate the barrel-vaulted ceiling, helping to showcase the original construction. At the service court, a second sand collector will be repurposed to house a heat pump, plumbing utilities, exhaust ducts, and electrical conduits. The conduits will run along the vaulted ceiling, creating a new grid that mimics the original filtration system, a nod to its history.

The Public Folly's integration of light is also two-fold, with direct light during the day and supplemental electrical light at night. Similarly, META-Project uses

Looking up at the inserted light boxes in Public Folly

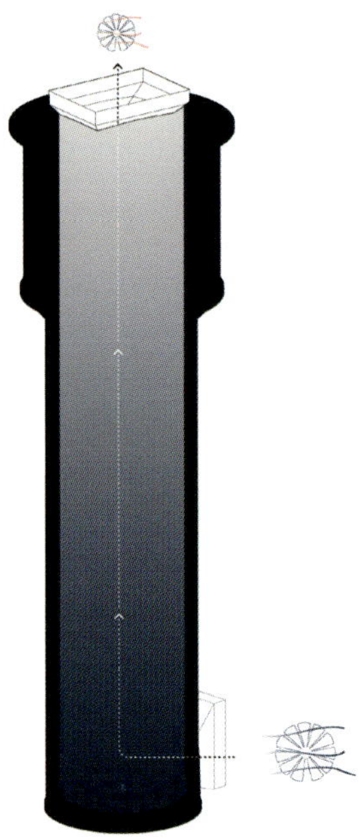

Ventilation

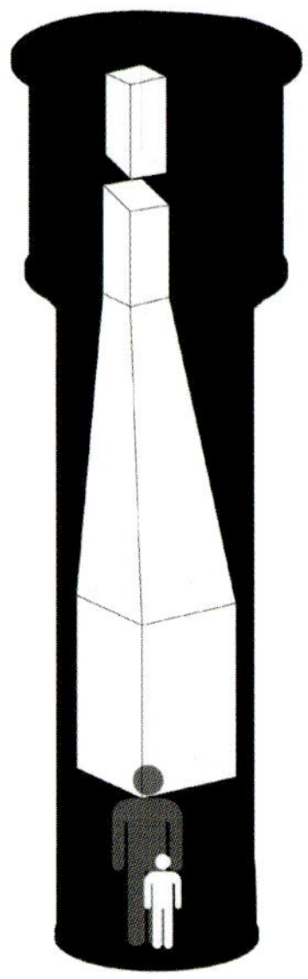

Proportions

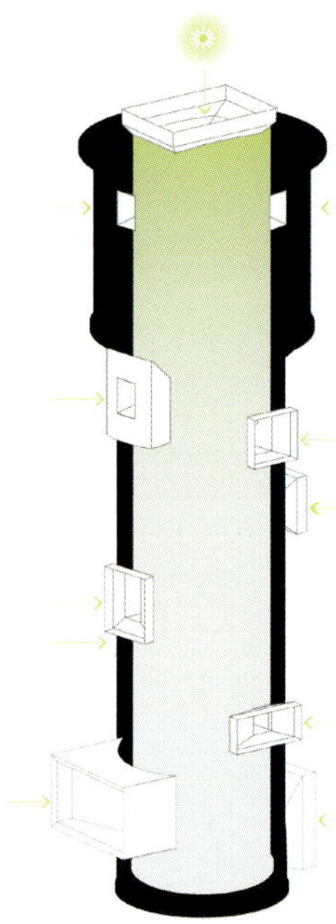

Sunlight

the existing windows, with only minor alterations, for light supply. To maximize the light quality, a viewing deck and five light boxes are introduced, which directs daylight into the expansive cylinder. Reinforced with steel funnels that are inserted into the windows' frames, these extensions are placed with intent and expand outward, making each light box seem larger than it really is. This design increases the exterior surface area, thus maximizing the amount of sunlight that reaches the interior cylinder. Each of the six openings is treated with a different monochromatic scheme, which creates a brilliant array of colored light within. At the top of the water tower, a singular light tunnel is inserted to help reflect daylight from above down to the entrance. Additionally, the Public Folly is designed to emit light outwards and become a beacon viewed from afar. At night, the monochromic light boxes create bursts of floating color while the water tower's masonry form disappears into the darkness. The supply of electricity to the light boxes is made possible by the insertion of an interior skin within the tower. Undisruptive to the original structure, a series of electrical conduits run within this new wall and supply the various light boxes with electricity for evening luminance. By using the properties of a funnel to maximize and distribute light on both the interior and the exterior, META-Project transforms this infrastructural monolith into a public space and community icon.

Stand Up Tall: Proportional Space

While water takes on the form of its container, humans are not as flexible. Driven by the need for minimal clearances, architectural codes are implemented to create space that is comfortable and accessible for all. But because water's infrastructure is only accessed during maintenance, there are no regulations for those dimensions. While some infrastructure is more generous than others, most structures are designed only for operational efficiency. Minimal vertical height and massive wall thickness are common architectural features that lead to cramped quarters. For these areas to be converted into spaces for human use, various forms of expansion have been implemented to create the appropriate proportions.

For its first 80 years of existence, the McMillan Slow Sand Filtration site remained below ground, hidden by a beautifully landscaped park. During construction, the topography was dramatically altered by a cut and fill operation. Across the entire site, the extent of re-grading varied from a 12-foot depression at the northern end, to a 16-foot infill at the southern end. As a result, the filtration cells have minimal interior height, but their horizontal width is endless, encompassing one acre. This extreme variance between cell width and height demands vertical expansion. To achieve this, the existing column grid will be broken and an alternate structure inserted to help disperse the concrete vaults' lateral loads. This intervention will be made up of steel cubes

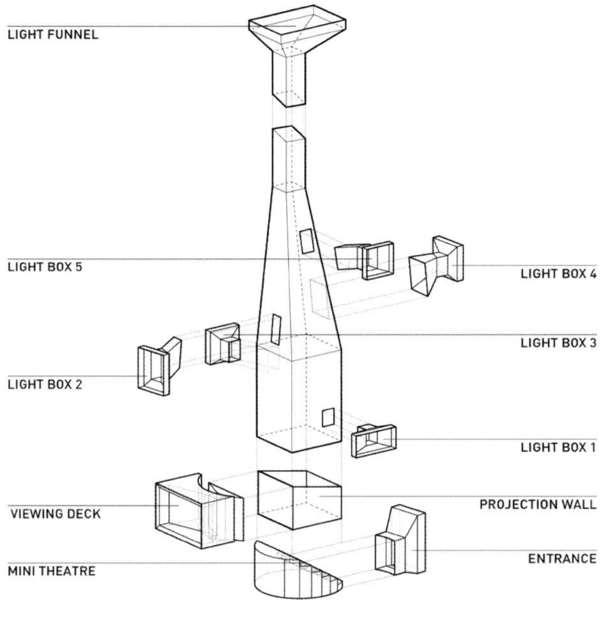

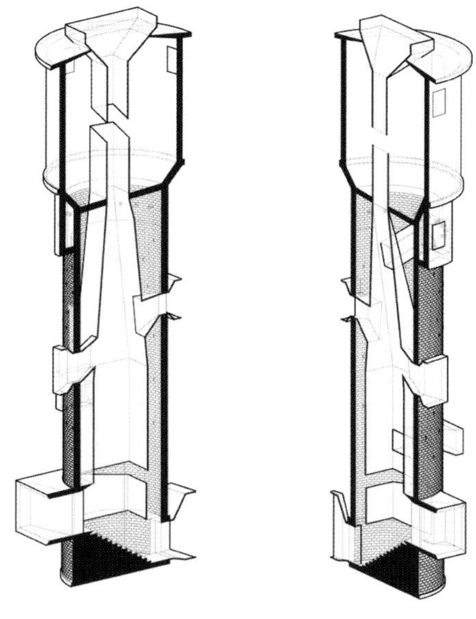

that will be elevated off of the sand and rested on the existing column's footing. Acting like a grid within a grid, these steel cubes create zones of uninterrupted space through the removal of 14 x 14 foot sections. When grouped together, larger spaces form and their additional height alter the landscape above. The result is a split-level plan that expands vertically for various levels of activity below. With the introduction of more proportional space, the DC Exchange will create harmony between old and new architecture through vertical expansion and surface manipulation.

The inherent characteristics of a water tower are centered on the properties of verticality, allowing gravity to play its natural role. Proportionally, this creates a disconnect between extreme height and minimal width. Although the Public Folly expands horizontally, with the insertion of the light boxes, its main alteration is in the vertical plane. Due to its extensive height, the Public Folly uses perspective to create space. META-Project inserts a double-ended funnel that spans the height of the water tower, creating endless depth. This funnel focuses one's view upwards and outwards, rather than within the water tower's confined walls. At the base of the tower, a series of steps help to connect Public Folly's entrance to the interior viewing deck. In terms of square footage this deck is small, but its visual connection with the outside creates the illusion of expansive interiors, blurring the space contained within the water tower with the exterior. While the Public Folly is only a single floor, META-Project utilizes the circulation space, helping to expand the limited square footage of the tower. Although the steps' primary use is circulation, they also function as seating to create a mini-theater within the tower's walls. This approach of maximizing all areas inside the water tower allows the interior to feel larger without expanding the original walls. Through the technique of perspective, META-Project adds proportional space within this obsolete water tower.

Move In

When infrastructure can no longer serve its purpose, it becomes obsolete. More often than not, infrastructure's robust structures surpass its technological relevance, leaving vacant core and shells buildings behind. In order to reactivate these spaces, occupancy is necessary. Through the incorporations of human needs: light to navigate, air to exist and proportions to inhabit, an industrial form can be converted into a multiuse community facility.

Water's infrastructure is a unique typology, which causes difficulty with structural reuse. But through adaptation its lifetime can be extended for years into the future. Whether its built form is contained below ground or elevated in the sky, or its space is constricted by minimal height or limited by finite width, these characteristics can be altered through a myriad of creative

LEFT
Exploded diagram of interventions
RIGHT
Sectional axonometric views

TOP

Sand pits at the McMillan Slow Sand Filtration Site

BOTTOM

Section through the DC Exchange, a proposed conversion of the McMillan Slow Sand Filtration Site

ways. With the integration of proper ventilation, daylight and proportional space, infrastructure built to contain, treat or distribute water can be repurposed for contemporary use.

ENDNOTES:

1 Steven J. Burian; Nix, Stephan J.; Pitt, Robert E.; and Rocky S. Durrans. "Urban Wastewater Management in the United States: Past, Present, and Future". *Journal of Urban Technology*. Volume 7, issue 3 (2010): pages 33-62, https://dx.doi.org/10.1080%2F713684134.

2 Mark Cartwright, "Aqueduct – Definition." *Ancient History Encyclopedia*. 1 September 2012. http://www.ancient.eu /aqueduct/ (accessed September 5, 2016).

3 EHT Traceries, Inc. "McMillan Slow Sand Filtration Plant." *Historic Preservation Report for the Proposed Redevelopment of the McMillan Slow Sand Filtration Plant*, July 28, 2010, Final Draft.

4 Stanley Greenberg. Invisible New York: The Hidden Infrastructure of the City (London: The Johns Hopkins Press Ltd, 1998)

5 Douglas Harper. "Infrastructure." *Online Etymology Dictionary*. http://dictionary.reference.com/browse/infrastructure (accessed January 10, 2014).

6 Eric Hobsbawm. The Age of Revolution: Europe 1789-1848 (United Kingdom: Weidenfeld & Nicolson Ltd. Vintage Books, 1962).

7 Thorkild Jacobsen, and Seton Llyod. Sennacherib's Aqueduct at Jerwan (University of Chicago Press: Oriental Institute Publication, 1935), page 24.

8 META-Project. "Public Folly — Water Tower Renovation PR Text." Dongcheng District, Beijing: August 5, 2013.

9 META-Project. "Water Tower Renovation — Industrial Heritage Reuse." December 2012. http://www.meta-project.org/projectdetail?projectQueryCon.id=47&select=2,1 (accessed September 3, 2016).

10 Leonard Metcalf; and Eddy P. Harrison. "American Sewerage Practice." *Design of Sewers*. Vol. I, (1914).

11 "Public Folly - Water Tower Renovation / META — Project." *ArchDaily*. August 20, 2013. http://www.archdaily.com/417034/public-folly-water-tower-renovation-meta-project/ (accessed September 3, 2016).

12 "Reference Terms — Infrastructure." *ScienceDaily*, 2006. https://www.sciencedaily.com/terms/infrastructure.htm.

13 J. C. Rodda and Lucio Ubertini. The Basis of Civilization — Water Science? (International Association of Hydrological Sciences, 2004).

14 Cady Staley; and George S. Pierson. The Separate System of Sewerage, Its Theory and Construction (New York: Van Nostrand, 1899).

15 Su Chen; Fang Chun. *Water Tower Renovation*. December 2012. http://www.meta-project.org/projectdetail?projectQueryCon.id=47&select=2,1. Accessed September 2016.

16 Lewis Francis. *McMillan Sand Filtration Plant*. June 2014. Accessed October 2016.

17 Victoria Perking. *McMillan Sand Filtration Site*. May 2012. Accessed October 2016.

18 Thomas Jacobus. *McMillan Sand Filters, Washington, DC.* 1902. Corps of Engineers, Office of Washington Aqueduct, DC. Accessed October 2016.

THE TEARS OF THE U.S.S. ARIZONA

A TOMB THAT LIVES

by ALEXANDER FORD AND NICHOLAS GERVASI

The Site

The history of the Japanese attack on Pearl Harbor and the U.S.S. Arizona have been thoroughly treated by scholarship. This paper will refrain from repeating the historical narrative, but instead offer a short outline of events, and aim to engage a wider sense of recollection. Since the U.S.S. Arizona sank 75 years ago, her ruins have been leaking oil into the harbor, a phenomenon colloquially referred to as the "Tears of the Arizona." Within our lifetime, the oil reservoirs that remain on board will empty. Our aim is to reconsider the traditionally static role of the monument as an object of architecture, and to propose by way of incorporating the seawater into a hypothetical design proposal, a building that is both alive and operates as an extension of the wreckage condition, as opposed to a rhetorical projection of it. By viewing the submerged wreckage as an opportunity for monumental adaptive reuse, and by situating the remains of the U.S.S. Arizona in the context of experimental preservation, the morphology of the monument — the program of reverence, memory, and cultural signification--transforms into a question: Can the Tears of the Arizona be preserved? The U.S.S. Arizona, a Pennsylvania Class battleship no. BB-39, set off on her maiden voyage in June of 1916. As early as 1927, the Japanese Navy War College had begun examinations of a hypothetical attack centered around Pearl Harbor. In 1928, Captain Isoroku Yamamoto lectured on the subject.[1] By 1940 Yamamoto's proposed attack on Pearl Harbor had been suggested and rejected on more than one occasion. It was only by threat of resignation, not just by Yamamoto but by the entire staff of representatives of his Combined Fleet, that Yamamoto's plans were finally approved in October of 1940.[2] Just before dawn on December 7th, 1941, 353 Japanese aircraft launched from the decks of Yamamoto's four heavy carriers, including 40 torpedo planes, 103 level bombers, 131 dive bombers, and 79 fighters.[3] The attack began at 7:55am and lasted only seventy-five minutes. 2,403 Americans were killed. A staggering 48.9% of those who died perished on the U.S.S. Arizona alone: roughly one in two.

The bombing of the U.S.S. Arizona was particularly catastrophic. Eleven minutes after the first blast, at 8:06am, an 800-kilogram bomb struck the front of Turret 2 and ricocheted forward toward the starboard side, puncturing the deck off-center between Turrets 1 and 2.[4] Seven seconds later, a colossal explosion tore the entire battleship in half. Within 9 minutes, the U.S.S. Arizona had sunk 40 feet to the bottom of the harbor. Resultant fires in the vicinity burned for two days. The shockwave from the blast that destroyed the Arizona was so strong that it whipped out the fires blazing on the deck of the Vestal, a repair ship moored nearby.[5]

Since the ship sank in the winter of 1941, the wreckage of the U.S.S. Arizona has been leaking oil at a steadily increasing rate into the open water at Pearl Harbor. The day before her demise, on December 6th, the Arizona was fully fueled and held 1.5 million gallons in preparation for a trip to the mainland, scheduled for the end of the month. While much of this oil fueled the fires and explosions which destroyed the ship, some 500,000 gallons still remained by the time the ordeal was over, and have been leaking from unidentified breaches in the hull interior for seventy-five years. The current rate of leakage is approximately two to nine quarts of oil per day.[6] In 1989, the National Park Service conducted research on the wreckage site and published an extensive historical and archaeological report which included figures pertaining to the hull corrosion and structural integrity.[7] While the National Park Service has since concluded that the amount of oil streaming into the bay poses no chemical hazard, there remains the fear that a catastrophic collapse of the hull structure might release all of the remaining oil at once, and do significant damage to the harbor and surrounding Hawaiian coastline.

Further, this incredible phenomenon — easily visible to the eye of an observer and occasionally in such large quantities as to appear even on satellite imaging — is temporary. The oil reservoirs housed within the confines of the Arizona's corroding hull are draining now faster than ever before, and soon the shimmering black scar draining from the tomb year-round will dry up entirely.

The Water

The existing monument on site at the shipwreck was designed by Alfred Preis, and completed in 1962. Preis was an Austrian-born architect who was detained at the start of the war in an internment camp on Sand Island, Honolulu, due to his foreign nationality, and considered an enemy of the country.[8] Following the war and his release, a competition for the memorial design was held by the U.S. Navy, which stipulated the structure be in the form of a bridge that spans the wreckage. Preis' design is a wholly metaphorical object, described in the form of representations and substitutions, of architecture for poetry and poetry for architecture. Preis' bridge scheme employs 21 apertures cut into the main observation deck to represent a 21-gun salute to the dead. It contains a characteristic sag in the center and stands tall at the ends, which the architect likened to the height of

A proposed monument that creates a registry of the leaking oil from the U.S.S. Arizona

American pride prior to the war, the depths of despair during the war, and the subsequent rise of American power that followed the war.[9] Critics at the time of the monument's dedication instead likened it to a crushed milk carton, and Preis' son, Jan Peter Preis, remarked that his father was outraged but maintained that the structure would be appreciated in time. However strong or weak any individual may come to decide such formal-conceptual connections are, the fact remains that in the water beneath, the Tears of the Arizona are draining quietly away into the sea and will eventually be only a memory.

Preservationists and conservationists are in the habit of considering natural forces and pollutants as destructive processes to objects. Put simply, environmental forces act to erode the object of note — constituting a base loss of material — and the attitude both employed and taught in this regard is usually to mitigate those forces of decay as much as possible. Unfortunately, this frame of mind renders the architecture of an object to be fossilized. That fossilization becomes the subject of apologetics targeted at characterizing the object in question as a purely didactic thing, as though the highest form of preservation is intimately tied to pedagogy. But architects have long been in the practice of welcoming and reinterpreting environmental pressures critically, incorporating the aesthetics of decay into the conceptual and material heart of the structure. One of the most prominent examples of such an approach is the renovation of the ground floor and gardens at the Querini Stampalia Foundation in Venice, by Carlo Scarpa. Designed to incorporate the Venetian canals, Scarpa elected to open the building to the canals that define the unique Venetian urban condition rather than keep the structure hermetically free of water. Scarpa's approach confronted and embraced the degradative effects of water on the architecture.

The Monument

The proposed monument elects to integrate the water that flows over the wreckage of the U.S.S. Arizona, creating a prefabricated, permanent registry of the leaking oil

The existing monument on site at the shipwreck, designed by Alfred Preis and completed in 1962

before the reservoir is emptied entirely. That registry of materials could then be extracted from the site and preserved independently of the building itself. In effect the architecture is tasked with the derivation and creation of an entirely new, eternal artifact from the transient, polluted condition on site.

As the original U.S. Navy design competition stipulated, the monument takes the shape of a bridge spanning the ruins of the ship, though instead of traversing the site, the bridge is oriented vertically along the length of it and anchored just off the prow. This composition allows the structure to work along the major axis of oil drainage observed on site, and perform as a collection vessel more effectively than would a transverse orientation. Along the port side of the ruins, seven concrete pylons are anchored to house seven salvaged Pennsylvania-Class aircraft-handling cranes, which in turn support the cantilevering armature from above as it spans the Arizona's hull and slopes downward into the water.

The entire structure is made of several prefabricated component parts, and could be assembled from the crane's superstructure, similar to how a tension bridge would be built. In section, the triangular profile provides less material than a square section and thus less weight as well as fewer points of connection to negotiate. Suspended by a network of floatation pistons tied into the central columns, a main platform sits level atop the surface of the water and provides the major route of access along the length of the hull.

The monument consists of three major rooms: First, an antechamber serving to dock the harbor ferry and bring visitors to and from the site. The antechamber is also the structural anchor point of the bridge armature. Second, a memorial room located directly over the spot between turrets I and II where the bomb that detonated the black-powder magazines punctured the deck. A submerged industrial planter houses a single cypress tree, which grows in the center of the memorial room, some twenty-five feet over the bomb's precise entry point. Third, at the end of the structure, as the depth of the water rises up to four feet, is located a small hypostyle hall comprised of 8-foot white travertine columns anchored into the bridge armature. The location of this open-ended memorial room serves to collect as much of the draining oil as possible and funnel the pollutants into the structure, where the travertine columns are to stain and blacken over a short period of time. In the future, when the Arizona's reservoirs are emptied, the columns themselves can be removed from the structure as a permanent registry of the Tears of the Arizona, and moved to a separate location where they would be placed under the tenure of a material conservation plan, and exhibited.

What is important in considering the decaying forces of pollution, corrosion, and erosion that are causing not only the deterioration of the Arizona's ruins, but would cause the deterioration of the monument as well, is to recognize that there is a temporal event on site reaching the end of its life-span. Rather than propose a wholly metaphorical connection between the whimsy of a particular form and some more palatable conceptual or poetic inclination, architecture might be considered as a mortal object itself. That is, a temporary construction, which was designed with its deconstruction firmly in mind. In order to preserve the Tears we thus propose an object not of metaphor, but one of metonym. Not of substitution, but of extension.

The story of architecture is the active process of producing an artifact that demands to be conserved. That a point of deconstruction is implicit in the construction of the armature means that the architecture is subject to the same temporal forces that threaten both the wreckage and the Tears. With respect to the monument, the incorporation of decay constitutes the making of a relic as opposed to the loss of one. Once the panels are stained, if they're left in the water they will be brined over and stripped of that texture again in time. The materials prepared and offered by the building must be collected from the water at the correct moment in order to be saved.

ENDNOTES:

1 Mark Stille and Adam Hook. Yamamoto Isoroku: Leadership, Strategy, Conflict (Oxford: Osprey, 2012), page 17.

2 Ibid.

3 Figures issued by the National World War II Museum, in part of the exhibition "The D-Day Invasions in the Pacific," December, 2001.

4 Paul Stillwell. Battleship Arizona: An Illustrated History (Annapolis: The Naval Institute, 1991), pages 267-78.

5 Ibid., page 228.

6 U.S.S. Arizona Preservation Project 2004, "Baseline Environmental Data Collection." http://128.146.17.149/previous-programs/Arizona/Legacy_2.html. (10 Decmber, 2016.)

7 Scott Henderson. "Submerged Cultural Resources Study, USS Arizona Memorial and Pearl Harbor National Historic Landmark." Santa Fe: Submerged Cultural Resources Unit, Southwest Cultural Resources Center, 1989.

8 Teresa Shapiro. "Arizona Memorial Seen as a Dedication to Peace." *Honolulu Star Bulletin,* (May 2002)

9 Ibid.

THE EDGE CONDITION

RE-USE OF INDUSTRIAL HERITAGE ON URBAN WATERFRONTS: A CASE OF LONDON'S SECOND RIVER

by GRAEME EVANS & NAOMI HOUSE

Introduction

The beginning of the twenty-first century has seen growing interest in how industrial heritage is considered — its contribution to our understanding of the past and its place in the evolution of landscapes and societies. Waterside architecture has a special place in cultural heritage, and in industrial heritage in particular. It offers an entry point to the waterways that fuelled both production and early mass transportation, as well as essential infrastructure to support the growth of urban populations through the provision of drinking water, sewage disposal and human-nature ecosystems. Buildings that originated as mills, pumping stations and factories have been gradually transformed into studios for artists, designers and digital industries, into arts centres and museums, as well as private residences, waterside restaurants and leisure facilities, as these previously 'private' industrial waterways open up for recreation, dwelling and commercial use.

The phenomenon of waterfront architecture has, since the 1980s, focused on high profile port, dock and lake/riverside cities — from Barcelona, Liverpool, London and Venice, to Boston, Baltimore, Toronto and Montreal[1], whilst these and cities such as 'Guggenheim Bilbao' also look to iconic new buildings to reimagine their post-industrial futures. More prosaic and everyday waterside sites seldom attract this attention and investment, as either visitor attractions or as 'aesthetic anchors' to larger redevelopment projects, whether commercial, housing or culture-based. However, huge tracts of riverside industrial sites lay largely undeveloped and/or under-appreciated — from central and

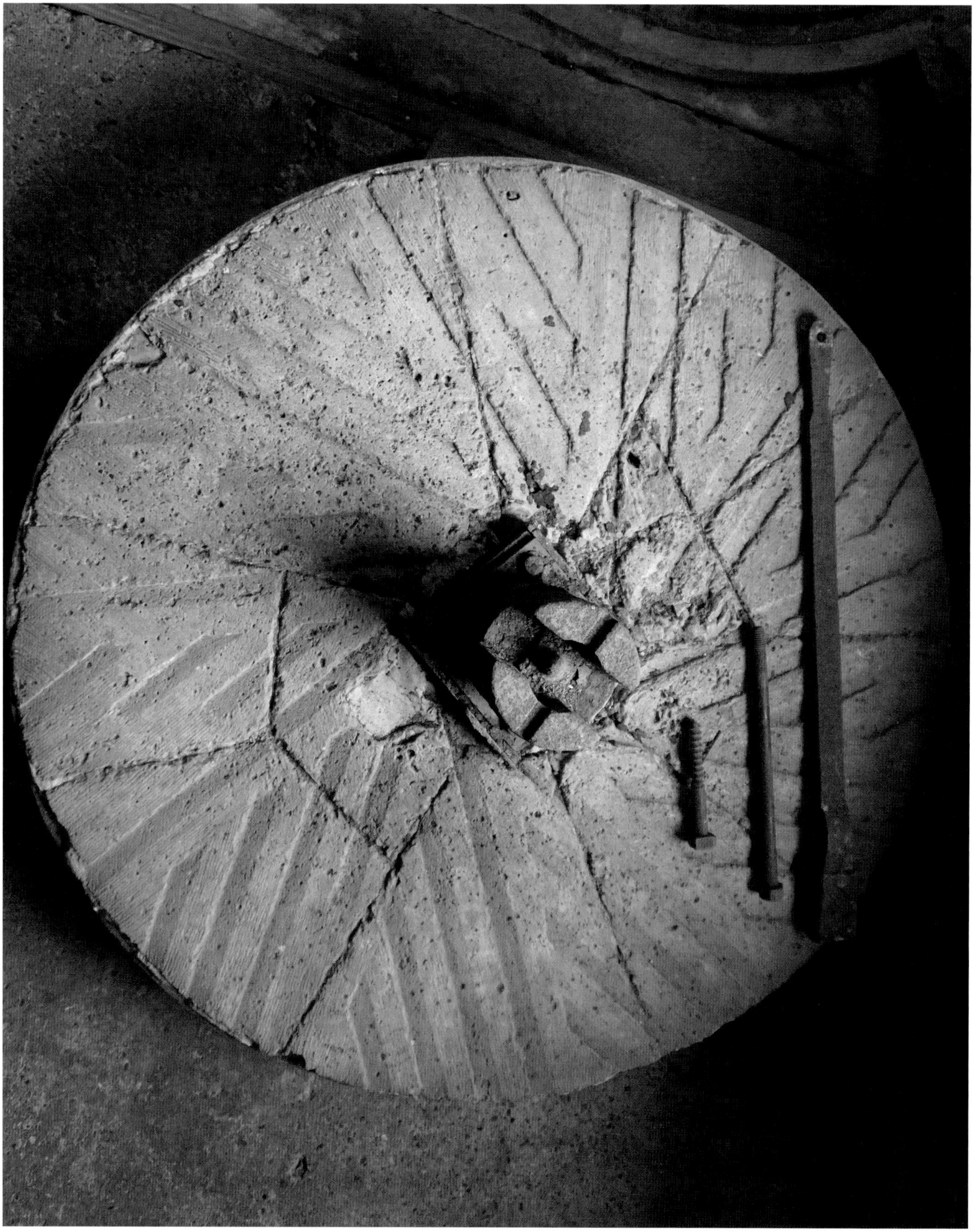

Millstones and wheels, House Mill at Three Mills Island

eastern Europe, North America, mainland China, to the 'hidden' rivers and canals which serve major cities such as London. However, continued population growth and demand for land and brownfield development for housing have started to make those waterfront areas that are more connected to major cities, more attractive for residential, culture-led regeneration and mixed-use development. These heritage buildings and sites also provide an important legacy of their industrial and cultural production past.[2] Their re-use nonetheless presents a challenge to viable redevelopment given the high costs of conversion — often listed historic buildings in conservation areas — the particular risks (and costs) associated with their waterside location, notably flood prevention and subsidence, and the limited options for re-use required in order to justify the capital investment and ongoing revenue support.

This article offers an investigation of the lower Lee Valley and the re-use of selected waterfront industrial heritage buildings. As an indication of the Lee Valley's amenity value and industrial heritage, over thirty mills are located on the river and Lee Navigation Canal, which today represent an important physical legacy and cultural heritage, alongside a network of locks and bridges. The river creates an edge condition, simultaneously linking and separating the surrounding landscape and framing our experience of this obsolescent infrastructure. These watery fragments of the past slip into view as you descend into the valley towards the River Thames, offering a glimpse of London's pasts, presents and possible futures. How might we identify an after-life for this strange environment? And what narratives can be suggested through the adaptive re-use of the waterfront architecture that persists? Water provides a medium for land and buildings, and mediates both as it flows over time and space, eroding and reshaping the built and natural environment as it goes.

Rewriting cultural identity

'If an original building is considered as a first discourse that conditions future formal discourses to be inscribed upon it, then remodeling can be conceived of as rewriting. . .as writing over, as underlining, as partially erasing, as interstitial writing (writing between the lines), as a way of qualifying, accentuating, quoting, commenting upon, as digression, interlude, or interval, as a way of writing parenthetically, of setting off by punctuation, as a new form for an old story.'[3] Within the context of urban regeneration and re-use it is useful to understand the Lee Valley as a palimpsest landscape both in terms of its topography and with regards to the architectural heritage that punctuates it — '...palimpsest landscapes...are not only the material expressions of physical and human processes at work over different spatial and temporal scales, they also capture aspects of the nonmaterial expressions of cultural identity and sense-of-place.'[4]

This intersection of landscape and architecture creates a complex and layered environment that is obsolete as a space of industry, yet vibrant as a place. The watery nature of this peculiar urbanity sustains it in a desirable continuum between past and present. The three sites that we encounter here all demonstrate a capacity to be rewritten, offering themselves up as spaces of intervention and re-use. Engaging with the material condition of the architecture, is it possible to isolate fragments that persist into the next iterations of use and inhabitation? The remnants of the erased, which are still visible here as traces, become clues — evidence perhaps of existing or passing design precedents; or clues to more traces as yet un-covered. In engaging with these sites forensically we operate as detectives, revealing the extraordinary instability, and potency of spaces and things.

Defining the Edge Condition

The River Lee, also known as London's 'hidden' or 'second river', originates in Marsh Farm in the Chiltern Hills north of London and flows for 50 miles south where it meets the River Thames at Bow Creek. With tributaries such as the 'New' River (constructed in 1613) 20 miles in length, or the Lee Navigation Canal a further 28 miles, the river feeds into 13 major reservoirs, which provide drinking water for a catchment area that extends over 500 square miles of flood plain. Several of these man-made reservoir areas are in the process of conversion to wetland 'nature' reserves incorporating visitor and interpretive education centres, making them open to the public for the first time.

The River Lee also provides a litmus test of London's industrial history and growth. Much of the City's manufacturing history is located here, plus agricultural production, which still serves London's population today. Industries such as gravel and mineral extraction, metalwork, ordnance (weaponry, e.g. Lee-Enfield rifle), early TV set production, the first plastic (Parkene), brewing, sweets factories, furniture-making, textiles, were all served by the working river transport system, the legacy of which is visible in wharf, mill and dockside buildings.[5] The Lee Valley has therefore been a source of innovation and industrial production throughout this time, now represented by creative industries, new housing and leisure developments on the revalorised waterfronts. Since the 1980s, an increasing number of artists have worked from studios along the river, attracted by their low cost, large loft style spaces and the promise of an alternative lifestyle/environment, as well as the inspiration derived from this watery post-industrial landscape.

The Lee Valley is also significant within the topography of London. Once the border between Viking and Saxon Kingdoms, today borough boundaries are drawn down the middle of the river with the left bank in a separate jurisdiction from the right. As a flaw in the urban landscape it separates and divides much of the

eastern reaches of the city from the rest of London. As an extended threshold, the Lee Valley is a place of otherness, where the water operates as an acoustic buffer zone, softening the edges of urbanity, and operating as a portal into another world. This liminal landscape represents what Solà-Morales describes as 'terrain vague' - 'strange places (that) exist outside the city's effective circuits and productive structures'[6]— a concept that Barron and Mariani extend — 'terrain vagues act variously as refuges, mirrors, and memento mori... As counter-spaces, terrain vagues are also containers of a fragmented shared history, illuminating the imperfect process of memory that constantly attempts to recall and reconstruct the past.'[7] Employing this metaphor we suggest that the Lee Valley is itself a terrain vague, simultaneously of London yet apart from it. Here the presence of the past is experienced as a heightening of the senses — a tuning in to the uncanny quality of place.

Towards a meaning of place

Norberg-Schulz describes the genius loci as the sense that people have for a place, while he considers the traditional form of buildings and cities as the basis for understanding this symbolic value.[8] As he later observes: 'the structure of a place is not a fixed, eternal state. As a rule places change, sometimes rapidly. [A]ny place ought to have the 'capacity' of receiving different 'contents'. . . A place which is only fitted for one particular purpose would soon become useless.'[9] Indeed the meaning of places should not reside with professionals alone, but with the people who have used, occupied and constructed their own meanings from them. As Bluestone maintains, 'we need a system for taking measure of and working with the reception side of cultural heritage . . . conservators can take an active role, however they also need to be open to the possibility that the places they conserve for one purpose may take on very different meanings over time.'[10]

In *The Secret Lives of Buildings*, Hollis suggests that 'The life of [a] building is both perpetuated and transformed by the repeated act of alteration and re-use.'[11] In practice, this alteration can be gradual or punctuate long periods of sustained single use (e.g. milling, pumping). In the waterside architectural re-use

White Building, Hackney Centre Wick

case studies reviewed here, the intermediate and planned adaptations have been conceived and executed with the input of former workers, such as retired dock-workers, millwrights (originally a specialized carpenter with knowledge of gear ratios, driveshaft speeds etc.), local historians, water utility workers and heritage volunteers who act as the stewards of, and interface with, the public over access to the sites. New occupants, notably practicing artists and architects, have also played an important role in the adaptation and usage of these buildings, particularly in the 'meanwhile' and self-build stage of their reincarnation and in the reinterpretation of their past. Students of Interior Architecture also provide a speculative insight into the possibilities of context-driven design projects, and this article incorporates schemes developed as part of final year work sited in these waterside heritage buildings.

Speculative Interventions

Using the lower Lee Valley as a site-specific context for a year-long study of the edge condition, a design brief looked to explore the complex social needs of incoming populations, and long-term inhabitants and businesses. Testing and exploring the potentially divergent needs of these groups, the proposals sought to accommodate either a duality of purpose through meantime projects, or to reconcile differing modes of occupancy and use through more permanent interventions. Testing the potential for new spatial typologies in this rapidly changing part of London, their attempts to address the edge condition revealed themselves through a range of interventions that often looked to exploit water, either as the focus of the project narrative, or as a contingent part of the urban landscape into which these narratives were inserted.

The three buildings that we focus on here all represent examples of spaces that have endured and experienced intensive historic industrial (including water utility) use, and change of use, followed by significant periods of redundancy and decline, and today, reoccupation and adaptation. And our reading of these places engages the slow look, utilizing peripheral vision to attend to the lost details of these environments. As Pallasmaa suggests, '[t]he very essence of the lived experience is moulded by hapticity and peripheral, unfocussed vision. Focussed vision confronts us with the world, whereas peripheral vision envelops us in the flesh of the world.'[12] Situated within 'an emergent forensic sensibility, an object-oriented juridicial culture immersed in matter and materialities,'[13] our analyses encounter the Lee Valley through the following buildings:

- The Marine Engine House at Walthamstow Reservoirs, 'Wetlands'
- The White Building on the Lee Navigation Canal, Hackney Wick
- Three Mills at Bromley-by-Bow on the River Lee

The Sinking Future Post Apocalyptic Flood Survival Centre

Adaptive Practices

The Marine Engine House, located between several Reservoirs at Walthamstow, is an example of Victorian civic utilitarian architecture. Constructed in 1894 as the Ferry Lane Pumping Station, it was designed by East London Waterworks Company's Architect, H. Tooley and Chief Engineer, Sir William Booth Bryan. The building is no longer in use and has been derelict for several years.

Consisting primarily of a two-storey building — the Engine House — with a single storey building attached to its northern side, there is a further parallel single storey building to the west, which includes the base of a now-demolished chimneystack.

Constructed in brick, the Engine House was designed in the simplified Italianate style much used for Victorian industrial buildings, with semi-circular heads to all of the principal door and window openings. There is also a relatively elaborate string course at mid-height and a highly detailed cornice to the two-storey section, with less elaborate details to the single-storey adjacent structures.

The roof of the Engine House is finished in plain clay tiles with extensive use of patent glazed rooflights and ridge lights in the single storey sections, and is pitched at around 45 degrees, half-hipped at its northern and southern ends. Doors and window frames are in painted softwood. Despite the missing chimney, and some external alterations, the building is still an imposing piece of Victorian industrial architecture. The Engine House, and the Pump Room at the extreme northern end of the building, both have interesting interiors — in the latter case this authenticity is enhanced by the remnants of its utilitarian past, with derelict equipment surviving redundancy prior to conversion.

These silent artefacts represent an important feature of industrial heritage 'consisting of remains of industrial culture which are of historical, technological, social, architectural or scientific value, including machinery, buildings, factories, mills, workshops, sites, mines, warehouses, stores.'[14] The renovation of the Marine Engine House plans to open up this abandoned edifice for the public and other users of the wetlands, transforming the Triple Engine Room, the Boiler House and the Turbine Room into a visitor centre, with exhibition spaces, education facilities and a cafe. The Marine Engine House is located at the centre of a new network of path and walks and the existing reed bed areas are being extended to diversify and increase the habitat, which, it is hoped, will attract a wide variety of new species to the site.

What is curious about the Marine Engine House, and indeed many of the buildings that extend through the Lee Valley, is that they were designed to house machinery and goods, rather than for human occupation. Adaptive practices read and interpret buildings in order to establish valid modes of intervention, but how can these practices respond to the material fragments of the past if these fragments bear witness to the sentience of objects rather than to the absent presence of human subjectivity?

The 'watery' fragments of the Marine Engine House that are imaged here evidence something akin to the 'vibrancy' of things, rather than human inhabitation, and suggest that objects and buildings have an agency independent of ourselves.

From the expansive reservoir and marshes of the Lee Valley, the river and canal system run south, supporting colonies of canal boats, waterside housing, residual industry, and parks and recreational areas. At Hackney Wick & Fish Island it bounds a long established urban settlement, an edge community descended from the former industrial and working river folk. Here a legacy of industrial buildings, wharfs and warehouses sits amongst largely social housing and new waterfront apartments, which have emerged as the East End docklands regeneration and transport system spread north up the Lee Valley.

The White Building, Hackney Wick, was built in 1897 by Clarnico, the confectioner, as a chocolate factory for the roasting and processing of imported cocoa beans brought from the docks by barge. Today the building serves as a mixed-use 'creative lab' with studio space for practicing artists, a residency space, community meeting room, an event space, and a waterside craft brewery & pizzeria. As Farley and Symmons observe: 'many and varied are the balconied canalside apartments and floating restaurants emerging from dark stretches of urban waterways.'[15]

From Fish Island, the canal and river run close together until they reach the tidal zone as the Lee finally flows into the River Thames at Bow. Here, Three Mills Island is located, built to exploit the ebb and flow of the river and driving a series of mills housed in a complex of buildings.

At the Three Mills Bow, the House Mill is a Grade 1-listed eighteenth century tidal mill set on the River Lee at Bromley-By-Bow in east London. The Mill was built on a pre-Domesday site in 1776, replacing an earlier mill located between two houses occupied by the miller and his family. Water mills were known in Roman times and were normally operated by the flow of a river. The Domesday Survey (the Domesday Book is a manuscript record of the "Great Survey" of much of England completed in 1086 by order of King William the Conqueror) recorded eight tidal mills in this area. They provided flour for the bakers of nearby Bow, who supplied bread to the City of London. In 1588, one of the two remaining mills was described as a gunpowder mill.[16] In 1728, Three Mills was bought by Peter Lefevre, a Huguenot, who operated the mills in conjunction with an adjacent distillery. The company also had its own carpenters, coopers and managed a large piggery fed on waste products gleaned from the mills various operations.

Built across the River Lee, the Mill operated by

trapping the sea and river water at high tide to turn the water wheels on the ebb. The outflowing water turned four large wheels driving twelve pairs of millstones. These four wheels and six of the pairs of millstones survive together with other historic machinery inside the building today.

The House Mill is now the oldest surviving and largest tidal mill in the UK and represents the qualities of both pre-industrial and industrial periods. Although milling ceased in 1941 after the area was bombed during the Second World War, the mill today functions as a low-key heritage visitor attraction with adjoining buildings occupied for film, theatre and creative industries — a growing typology of use for larger industrial heritage buildings, otherwise destined for private residential occupancy. A timber framed building, the House Mill, is clad in brick on three sides and has a doubled-ridged, steep roof with 12 dormer windows lighting its two attic storeys.

All buildings on the Three Mills site were partially restored and converted over a ten-year period by Julian Harrap Architects between 1989-1997. Minimal intervention led to sophisticated structural repairs to these timber frames using complex scarf joints and flitch plate reinforcement, including the repair and restoration of the fabric and the waterways below the building. The interior provides an insight to the world of the pre-turbine age of milling.

Water as a medium and mediator

In the three examples of adaptive re-use described, actual and speculative, water is both a medium — historically drawn to pump clean water for consumption, to drive millstones and transport raw materials for manufacture — and also a mediator between land and water, between territories or 'edges', and between time and space. On the one hand, the sense of place that these architectural representations evoke offers an insight to their utilitarian past, whilst their adaptation — pragmatic, functional and speculative — seeks to engage with present and future uses, and the values attached to these waterside structures. These buildings and their locales can be seen as heterotopian,[17] rather than understood in terms of a dialectical utopian/dystopian conflict between nostalgia and sentimentality, and decline through redundancy, neglect and gentrification. In this sense, their flexiblity and fluidity, where water again defines their re-use through wetlands nature reserve, mill heritage centre, or post-industrial creative industrial workspace, reveal their palimpsest nature, but this layering leaves enough in each case to detect the traces and meanings from their past purpose and heritage.

ENDNOTES:

1 Richard Marshall, Waterfronts in Post-Industrial Cities (London: Spon, 2001)

2 Graeme Evans, "The Lee Valley: an industrial river system and heritage landscape". In *Patrimonie Paesaggi : Costruiti Dall'acqua*. Edited by Margherita Vanore, Milano: Mim Edizioni Srl-Udine, 2016, (90-101).

3 Rodolfo Machado, "Toward a Theory of Remodelling — Old Buildings as Palimpsest", *Progressive Architecture*, 11, 76, (1976), 48

4 Jasper Knight, "Development of Palimpsest Landscapes", 2012, http://serc.carleton.edu/68942, accessed 16 December 2016.

5 Jim Lewis, London's Lee Valley: Britain's Best Kept Secret (Chichester: Phillimore & Co), 1999.

6 I. De Solà Morales, "Terrain Vague". In *Anyplace*, Edited by Cynthia C. Davidson, Cambridge, MA: MIT Press, (1995), 118-123.

7 Patrick Barron and Manuela Mariani, Terrain Vague: Interstices at the Edge of the Pale (London: Routledge, 2013), 1-2.

8 Christian Norberg-Schulz, Genius Loci: Towards a Phenomenology of Architecture (New York: Rizzoli, 1985), 33–35.

9 Christian Norberg-Schulz, "The phenomenon of place", in Kate Nesbitt, ed., *Theorizing a new agenda for architecture: an anthology of architectural theory 1965-1995* (New York: Princeton Architectural Press), 1996, 422.

10 Daniel Bluestone, "Challenges for Heritage Conservation and the role of Research on Values" In: *Values and Heritage Conservation*, edited by Erica Avrami, Randall Mason, Marta de la Torre (Los Angeles: The Getty Conservation Institute, 2000), 67.

11 Ed Hollis, The Secret Lives of Buildings: From the Parthenon to the Vegas Strip in Thirteen Stories (London: Portobello Books), 2010.

12 Juhani Pallasmaa, The Eyes of the Skin (Chichester: J. Wiley & Sons, 1996), 10

13 Eyal Weizman, Forensic Architecture: Notes from Fields and Forums, Kassel: *Documenta* Series 062, 13.

14 TICCIH (The International Committee for the Conservation of the Industrial Heritage), Industrial Heritage Re-tooled: The TICCIH guide to Industrial Heritage Conservation. Lancaster: Carnegie. 2012, p.236.

15 Michael Symmons Roberts & Paul Farley, Edgelands (London: Vintage, 2012), 118.

16 Brian Strong, "A tidal mill tale", *Journal of the Islington Archaeology & History Society*, 4, 1 (2014), 16 –17.

17 Michael Foucault, "Of Other Spaces: Utopias and Heterotopias", *Architecture, Mouvement, Continuité*, 5, 1984: 46 – 49.

BACK TO THE FUTURE

THE SPATIAL DIMENSION OF WATER MANAGEMENT

by KEES LOKMAN

"From the inception of our species, coping with the availability — or unavailability — of water resources has been an essential element of human beings' strategies for survival and well-being. Throughout history human ingenuity was manifest in the means by which water was procured, transported and allocated to various uses. The quality, distribution, seasonality and amount of water have been key determinants of subsistence, health and settlement potentials."
(Hassan 2011: 14)

Water management is essential to human development. Throughout history, reciprocal relationships between water management, human settlement, food production, climatic conditions, and social organization—on both local and regional levels—have produced a range of physical landscapes with a myriad of social-ecological and spatial dynamics. More recently, technological advancements coupled with accelerated processes of urbanization and agricultural production have created new demands for water, as well as new approaches to wastewater management and flood control. As such, today, we are confronted with multiple dimensions of water management—operating across various spatial and temporal scales.

In this context, the twentieth century was primarily characterized by a command-and-control attitude towards water management. Often sponsored by state governments through large-scale infrastructure developments (i.e. irrigation works, hydroelectric dams, and so on), these projects have favored the notion of

The Big U is one of the winning projects of Rebuild by Design. It combines a continuous 10-mile long flood protection infrastructure along Lower Manhattan with new open sapces and public programs to benefit surrounding communities

hydraulics (engineering) over hydrology (ecological processes). Not surprisingly, the cumulative effects of these interventions have triggered drastic changes to (river and coastal) ecologies, built environments, people's livelihoods and geopolitical relationships (Lokman 2016a). With the realities of climate change, ongoing urbanization and environmental degradation, there is an urgent need to develop adaptive planning approaches, policies and spatial strategies to manage water.

In recent decades, several of such new water management concepts have been proposed, including: *integrated water resources management, adaptive management,* and, more recently, the *water–energy–food nexus* (Giupponi and Gain 2016). And while these frameworks certainly help to elevate the debates on water management, they primarily focus on the use of planning tools and policy mechanisms to enact change. The role of design and the inherent spatial dimensions of water, however, remain largely overlooked. Roggema (2009: 59), in discussing climate change and its consequences for water management and energy developments, states: "The adaptation to climate change is well represented in strategies, policies and the media…but integrated designs for adapted spatial plans are hardly available. This is curious, because adaptation to climate change needs to be implemented and realized mainly through spatial patterns and layout." In other words, there should be more emphasis on the translation of policies into spatial design strategies in order to shift people's ways of thinking, and to make visible how the world can look by offering new ideas and formulating physical solutions to complex issues.

Along these lines, Priscoli (1998: 623) argues: "The spatial and functional characteristics of the river basins influenced human settlement and interaction long before the idea of the river basin started to be formalized into legal and administrative terms." Priscoli emphasizes water management has an inherent socio-spatial character which has evolved over time and space. We can learn from history in order to study how spatial, technical, and managerial solutions in the past can inform approaches to contemporary challenges such as sanitation, flood control and irrigation farming. As such, this article will focus on the interdependencies of people, water and space by discussing how we can manage water by actively co-designing with natural processes. How has water management historically informed the spatial configuration of landscapes? In which ways are these approaches incorporated in contemporary water management? Ultimately, how can we combine hard and soft-engineered water management practices to cultivate productive and dynamic social-ecological relationships?

The article begins by exploring three historical examples of water management, including: (1) the *chinampas* in Mexico City (a type of Mesoamerican agriculture which uses small, rectangular plots to grow crops); (2) Major John Wesley Powell's *drainage districts* (a proposal for an alternative hydro-political organization and water democracy for the American West); (3) the Dutch p*older model* (a mixed model of top-down and bottom up approaches to develop and maintain flood control infrastructure). Each example illustrates an approach to water management that fundamentally responds to local conditions, while embracing dynamic relationships between human agency and natural processes. Finally, the article discusses how these site-specific and culturally informed approaches are influencing contemporary water management projects.

Chinampas: A co-evolution of social and ecological processes

One of the most sophisticated ways of manipulating landscapes to manage water and grow food was developed in Mesoamerica, in an area now known as Mexico City. Founded by the Aztecs in 1325, Mexico City (then known as *Tenochtitlán*) is situated in the Basin of Mexico, a highland plateau with no natural drainage outlet. Until the late nineteenth century the Basin contained a network of shallow lakes, which fluctuated between 0.8 and 3.0m during dry and wet seasons (Sanders 1979). In order to control flooding, and to provide access to fresh water and food, the Aztecs developed an ambitious system of dikes, aqueducts, and *chinampas*: rectangular farming plots filled with fertile dredged sediments. This half-natural, half-artificial landscape was based on a dynamic stability between ecological processes, agricultural productivity, economic vitality and specific forms of social organization (Torres-Lima et al. 1994; Nichols at al. 2006, Lokman 2016b).

Chinampas provided the backbone of the Aztec Empire. When the Spanish invaded the region in the sixteenth century, *chinampas* covered an area over 1000 sq. km (Hassan 2011)—nearly a third of Rhode Island. Originally ranging from 6.0 to 9.0m wide and lengths of up to 100m, *chinampas* were constructed by alternating layers of dredged sediments and "thick mats of decaying vegetation" (Torres-Lima 1994: 38). A wattle fence and a planted row of native willows (Salix Bomplandiana L.) helped to retain soil and stabilize the edges. Once matured, the trees helped to block wind and trap warm air, permitting year-round cultivation and providing additional crop protection. The continuous application of animal manure, mud, and water from the drainage and transportation canals enhanced soil fertility and soil humidity, improving the overall growing conditions (Parsons 1991). This recycling of nutrients and waste not only reduced environmental impacts, but increased biological interdependence between crops and pest, and improved crop productivity, creating a highly complex and sustainable agro-ecosystem (Torres-Lima et al. 1994).

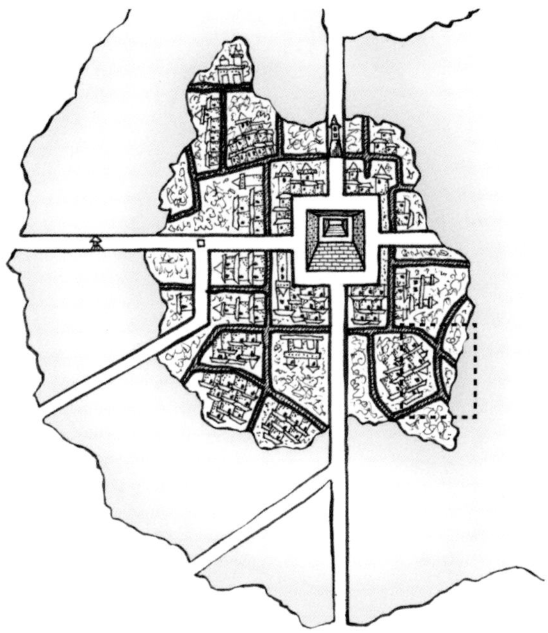

Tenochtitlan & Logo de Texcoco
1500 CE

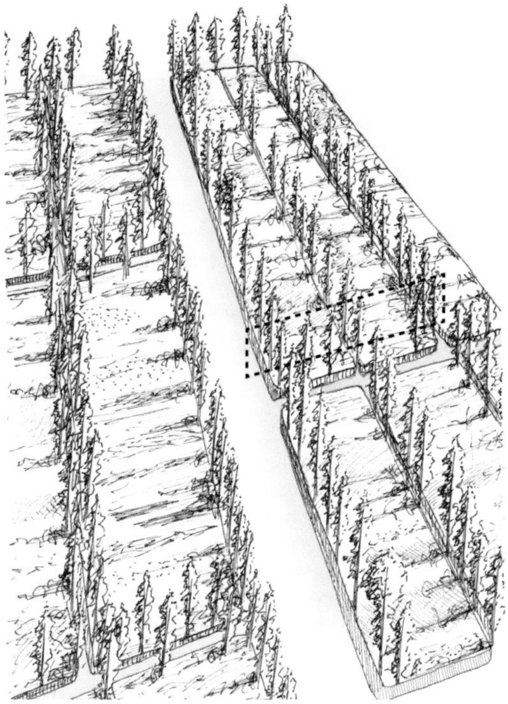

Chinampa Aerial

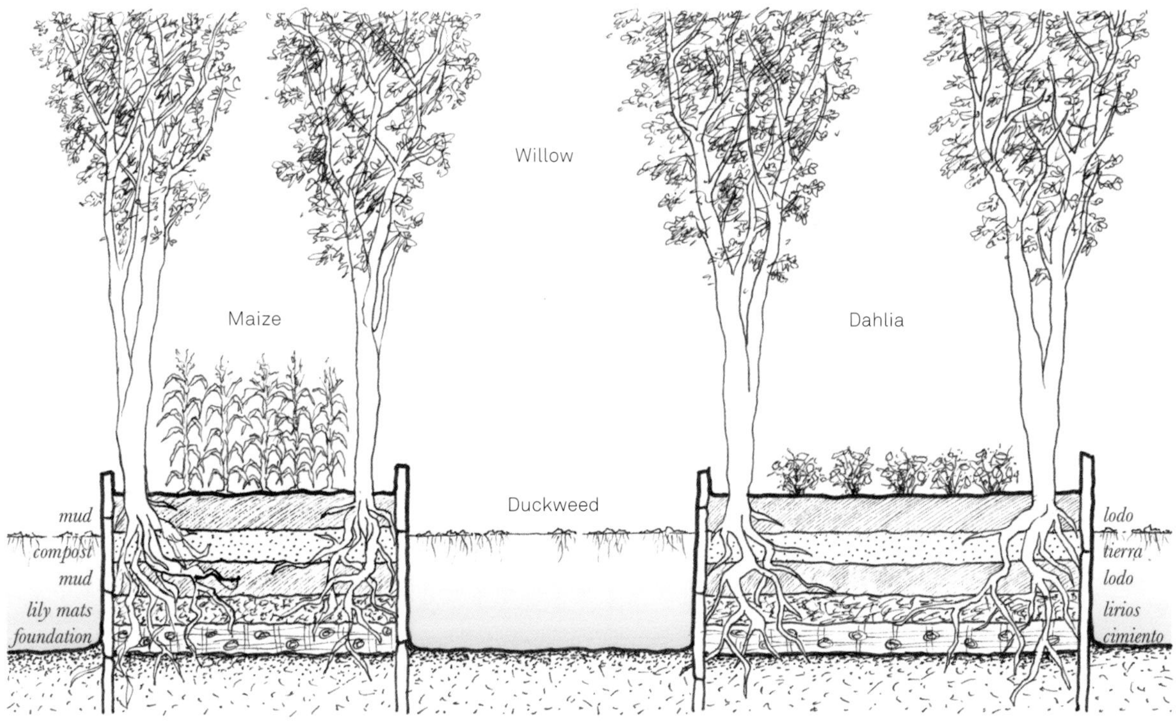

Chinampa Section

Illustrations of the chinampas system

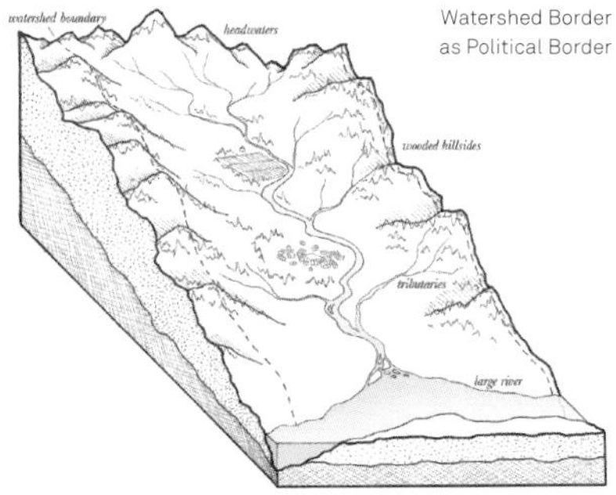

Watershed Border as Political Border

Watershed Democracy

Inherently shaped by the co-evolution of social and ecological processes, the distinct spatial configuration and sectional qualities of *chinampas*, in combination with centuries-long human stewardship, cultivated a heterogeneous landscape with numerous ecosystem services, including food provisioning, aquifer recharge, flood control, carbon storage, climate regulation, as well as providing critical habitat for numerous endemic and migratory species (Merlin-Uribe et al. 2013). Due to their spatial and functional complexity, *chinampas* were able to adjust to many different environmental and socio-economic pressures over time (Torres-Lima et al. 1994). In contrast to contemporary farming practices, which are mechanized and require large inputs of water and fertilizers, *chinampas* represent a low-tech and scalable form of agriculture based on closed-loop systems attuned to local ecological conditions. Moreover, they provided a diverse set of uses—from agriculture to housing, livestock keeping and recreation. And while only a few pockets of this pre-colonial agro-ecosystem remain today, the *chinampas* remain an inspiration in terms of developing sustainable methods of water management centered on the co-evolution of human systems and ecological processes.

Watershed Democracy: A communal way of water management

The next example focuses on John Wesley Powell's proposal for establishing *hydrographic basins*—political units defined by climate, topography and the natural flow of water. This idea not only promoted a communal way of managing water on a regional scale but also introduced a radically different way of organizing the territory of the American West—both spatially and politically.

Powell (1834–1901) was a geologist, explorer and conservationist. Through his many expeditions of the West, which is characterized by limited rainfall, high temperatures and poor soils, he understood that the political and jurisdictional systems governing water rights and natural resources in this part of the continent could not follow the conventional logic at the time. In 1878, he published the "Report on the Arid Lands of the United States," which recommended that none of the water should be privatized; it belonged to everyone within a specific "hydrographic basin," or what we now call a *watershed*. According to Powell, water rights should be tied to the land, and not be sold except along with deeds to the land.

Counter to the 19th century frontier mentality, Powell opposed common practices that allocated parcel, county and state boundaries based on Euclidean geometry. Instead, he suggested dividing the land based on topographic features, thereby establishing "irrigation districts"; small tracts of irrigable lands in the lower lying areas, and "pasture districts"; larger livestock ranches for grazing nearby springs and small streams (Powell 1878). From the forests on the upper slopes, the grazing lands at mid elevations, and the arable bottomlands, residents were to work together across the basin to establish regulations for the use of water for irrigation and subdividing the land. Privileges to mineral rights (and the use of water and timber for mining) would be managed by the United States in order to prevent powerful individuals to obtain single control over these resources. Beyond this, government had no role: communities should be left to control their own water resources and production.

Moreover, as second director of the US Geologic Survey (1881–1894), Powell also developed important new knowledge and spatial information. His team created an extensive inventory of maps in order to visualize America's geography—its watersheds and the inherent relationships between climate, physiography, soils and hydrology (Worster 2009). Using these scientific assessments, along with detailed studies of indigenous and Mormon irrigation systems (Lewis and Torbenson 1990), Powell estimated that only a fraction of the West could ever be effectively irrigated. He predicted that misalignment of socio-political boundaries and hydrographic regions would result in geopolitical conflict and unsustainable water management. Powell said: "I tell you, gentlemen, you are piling up a heritage of conflict and litigation over water rights, for there is not sufficient water to supply these lands."

Illustrations of political border following the regional watershed boundaries

In an era that encouraged expansionism and individualism, Powell advocated for cooperative stewardship, conservation and environmental planning. The *watershed* would serve as the foundation for a resilient sociopolitical and place-based organization of the West by instilling uniquely democratic principles and Jeffersonian ideals. Unfortunately Powell's recommendations were never adopted, and today, his words could not be more true. California, after witnessing the worst drought in its history, is currently facing extreme rainfall and flooding. The recent failure of Oroville Dam highlights the challenges of America's ageing flood control infrastructure. At the same time, the West is facing increased tension and disputes among municipalities, governments, farmers, environmental groups, industries and Native Americans over water allocation and management. With the implications of climate change, ongoing urbanization and environmental decline, now more than ever, it is important to revisit Powell's ideas, and envision new socio-spatial frameworks for managing water.

The Dutch Polder Model: Designing with water

The final precedent concerns the Netherlands, where a long-standing relationship with water has informed innovative adaptation strategies and a distinct sociopolitical attitude characterized by consultation, compromise and consensus, also known as the Dutch '*polder model*' (de Vries 2014).

With nearly a third of the country situated below sea level, integrated solutions to water management have always been important to the Netherlands (Lokman 2016c). Dating back as far as the 9th century, the Dutch began building dams, dikes and other flood control measures to protect settlements, agricultural areas, and reclaimed areas of land. While initially a primarily local matter, with the growth of cities and their hinterlands it became increasingly important to coordinate flood control among various stakeholders (de Mul and van den Berg 2011). This meant people and social classes living in the same '*polder*' (a reclaimed area of land protected by dikes) had to work together to fund, build and manage appropriate flood control infrastructures (van Tielhof 2015). Over time, they established '*water boards*' (regional water authorities) to coordinate flood protection, preserve water quality, and to manage the general water economy of their respective regions. These water boards are one of the first forms of public administration, and the oldest form of democratic government in the Netherlands (Dutch Water Authorities 2015).

Since water-related tasks are of existential importance to the Netherlands, the organizational structure of water boards is decoupled from the political structure—they have their own administration, governing body and financial structure. As such, the budget for water management is not balanced against that of health care, education, defense spending, and so on (Dutch Water Authorities 2015). Water boards also maintain an *interest-say-pay* principle: the higher the interest of a stakeholder, the more tax is raised. In return, these stakeholders will have more influence on decision-making. As such, taxes differ substantially across the country.

In line with the emergence of a new ecological paradigm, including notions of complexity and resilience, the Dutch have recently changed their water management approach from focusing primarily on protection *against* flooding to working together with water. After major floods in 1993 and 1995, the government initiated the *Room for the River* program (2006-2015). The project focuses on increased flood storage and enhancement of the spatial quality. It consists of 39 distinct but interconnected local projects, which deploy numerous

Ruimte voor de wall
Rendering of the new bypass channel at Nijmegen and Lent

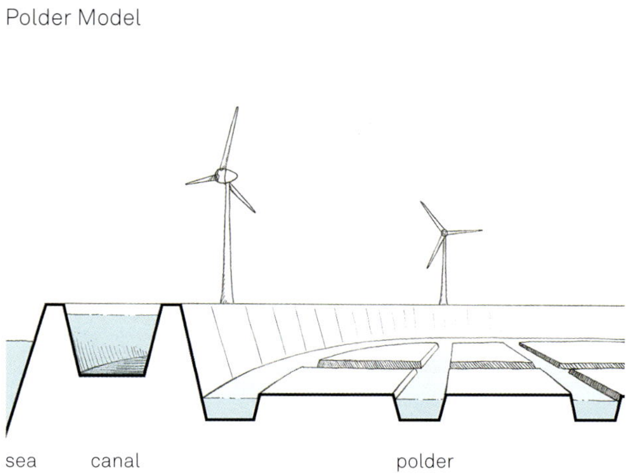

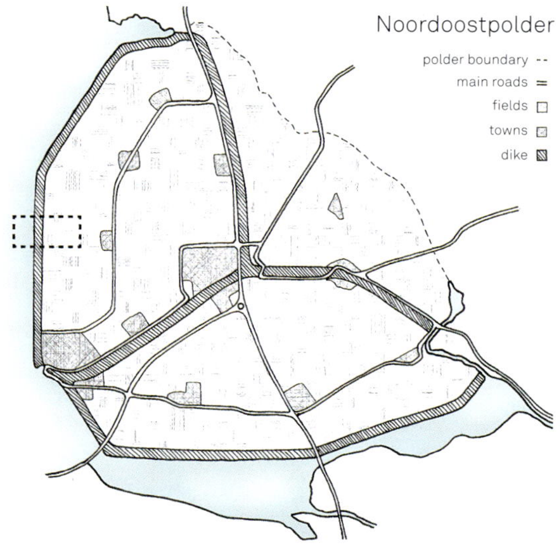

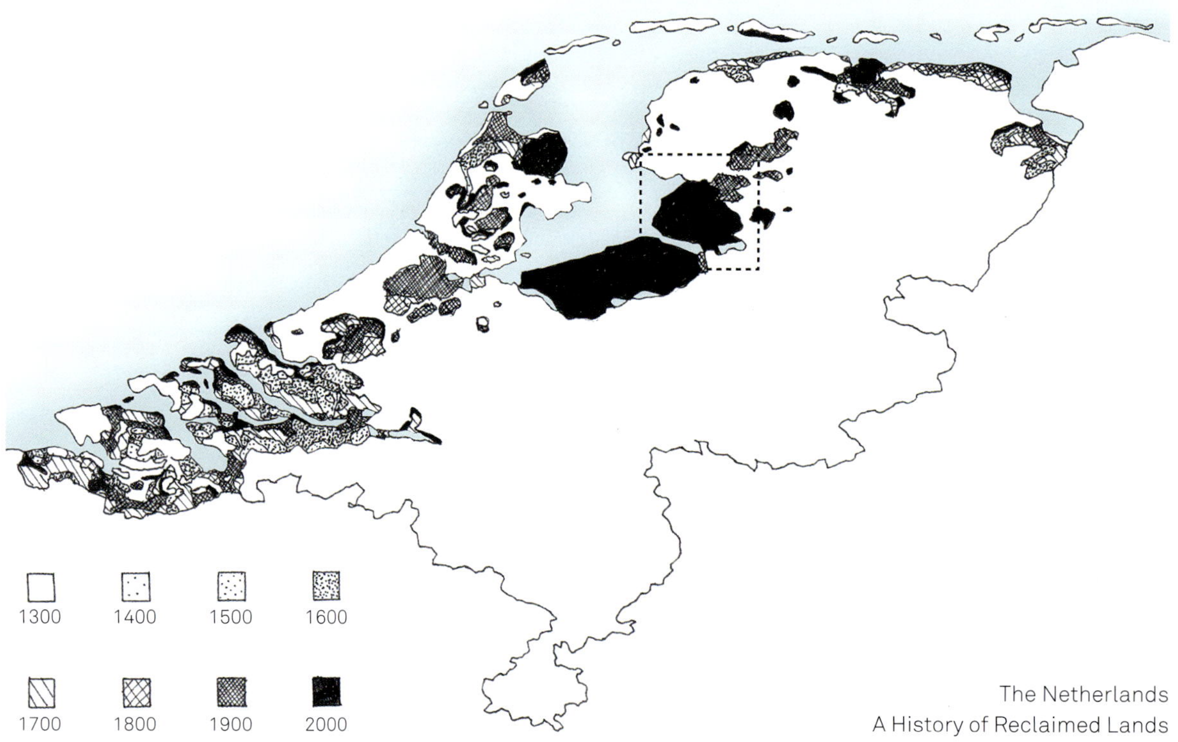

Illustrations of the contemporary Dutch Polder landscape

adaptation strategies and approaches, including depoldering (allowing water back into a polder), flood bypasses, dike setbacks and relocation of buildings to higher grounds. In addition to establishing extensive public participation platforms, the government also worked with various water institutes to develop a digital hydrologic model to calculate, coordinate and assess the overall effectiveness of all 39 projects.

Among the more visible projects is *Ruimte voor de Waal*, where a new bypass channel not only increased flood storage and provided habitat for fish and wildlife, it also created a new island with unique opportunities for recreation and urban development. Climate change and flooding are no longer seen as a risk but rather as a possibility to unlock new social, ecological and economic opportunities. As suggested by Veerman (2008: 7), "Changing the way our country is managed creates new options; working with water may improve the quality of the environment and offers excellent opportunities for innovative ideas and applications. Where there is water, new forms of nature can arise. Water can be used to produce food and generate energy. Flood defenses can be used for roads."

Moreover, these complex and multi-scalar spatial planning projects call for planning approaches that combine top-down policies with bottom-up participation. According to Jeroen Rijke et al., it is exactly "through application of a mixed centralized–decentralized governance approach, [*Room for the River*] has tackled governance pitfalls related to centralized planning approaches that previously impeded integrated water management" (Rijke et al. 2012: 379). Thus, while climate change is a serious challenge it is also provides preconditions for testing new planning frameworks, and for the design of dynamic, multifunctional landscapes.

Back to the Future

The examples discussed above illustrate sustainable water management that involve adopting practices capable of dealing with dynamic and ever-changing social-ecological conditions. They are based on notions of *co-designing* and *co-evolving* social and biophysical systems. As pointed out by Priscoli (1998: 623): "Increased interdependence through water sharing plans and infrastructure networks can be seen as increases of our flexibility and capacity to respond to exigencies of nature and reduce our vulnerability to events such as droughts and floods and thereby increase security." This also means, rather than holding on to a single approach to water management, we should develop a multiplicity of strategies and frameworks to solve issues of water scarcity, flood control, water governance and water ethics (Schmidt and Shrubsole 2013). This requires collaborative efforts and concerted action by all stakeholders in order to integrate knowledge and coordinate cross-boundary planning approaches.

Looking to the future, there are some reasons to be optimistic. The practice of landscape architects SCAPE, for instance, provides a good example of how mutualistic interactions between people, animals and plants (such were inherent to the *chinampas*) can be designed to create productive and resilient urban environments. In particular, SCAPE's *Oyster-tecture* project, which was commissioned by the Museum of Modern Art in 2009 for the Rising Currents exhibition, shows how humans, natural processes and marine animals can work together to create an ecological infrastructure that provides flood protection, habitat restoration, food, and recreation.

Located in Brooklyn, New York, the proposal harnesses the various qualities of oysters and other shellfish to construct new cultural and environmental relationships. Using a low-tech FLUPSY system (floating upwelling system), the oysters are nurtured in post-industrial Gowanus Bay, where they help filter and clean the water. Once matured, they are transferred to the intertidal zone of the Bay Ridge Flats. Here, the artificially seeded shellfish species are attached to an armature of fuzzy rope and old wharf piles to create a reef for aquatic species, birds and people. Over time, as sediment, plants and shellfish inhabit this constructed landscape, the reef becomes a living breakwater that simultaneously acts as a unique ecosystem and wave-attenuating armature to protect against storm surges and rising sea levels. The design-research for Oyster-tecture has informed multiple ongoing projects, including the proposal 'Living Breakwaters', which envisions a series of ecological infrastructures along the shores of Staten Island. The project recently received $60M from the U.S. Department of Housing and Urban Development (HUD) and is currently being implemented by the NY Governor's Office of Storm Recovery.

With respect to communal water management, the *acequias* in New Mexico present an alternative to current water-intensive and highly mechanized forms of agriculture in arid regions. While not a new invention (*acequias* have been around for centuries), both the social and spatial practices of the *acequia* culture can inspire novel ways of water management. Originally introduced by the Moors (North Africa), and further developed in Spain and former Spanish colonies, the term '*acequias*' refers not only to the physical irrigation channels but also to the social and organizational structure of a water-sharing network (Santistevan 2016). Construction and maintenance of the acequia system (canals, ditches, reservoirs) is done collectively (Lewis and Torbenson 1990). Engineered to use gravity and natural contours of the land, acequias divert snow runoff from a main river into an artificial network of channels to irrigate farming plots. The mother ditch (*acequia madre*) distributes water to lateral ditches

(*linderos*) and secondary laterals (sangrias) to irrigate specific fields. These ditches also help to restore aquifers and enhance habitats along riparian areas.

Acequia members (*parciantes*) elect a 'ditch boss' (*mayordomo)* who is in charge of managing the water and settling disputes. Together with the *acequia* community, the mayordomo is responsible for making sure all members meet their water needs for agricultural production throughout the season. As a non-capitalist form of farming and social relations, the *acequias* "call attention to alternatives in how societies can reproduce themselves materially, from households to the broader economy" (Gunn 2016: 91). The emphasis is on cooperation and sharing in order for each *acequia* member to leverage a certain level of material independence. Instead of seeking to generate profit, the motivation is to maintain a regenerative way of life between people and the land. The fact that water is still flowing through the *acequias* speaks to their socio-economic and spatial resiliency. With economic uncertainties and the implications of climate change (variation in available water supplies and crop yields), *acequias* provide an adaptive, resilient and democratic model to support small-scale agricultural practices in semi-arid and arid regions.

The area of water management which is perhaps most rapidly evolving concerns regional flood risk mapping as well as the development of new spatial planning and design strategies for sea level rise adaptation. After Hurricane 'Sandy' hit the New York Region in 2012, HUD launched the *Rebuild by Design* initiative to facilitate collaborations between transdisciplinary design teams and local communities in order to develop strategies that promote socio-economic opportunities within a framework of ecological resilience. With a focus on using a research-based and design-driven approach to problem solving, *Rebuild by Design* provided funding for ten teams to develop innovative approaches for those areas in the region most vulnerable to flooding. These teams, then, worked several months with experts, community and local government stakeholders to develop strategies that were both realistic and replicable. In 2014, HUD announced six winners—SCAPE's *Living Breakwater* being one of the winning proposals—which have received additional funding to further develop and implement their projects.

Rebuild by Design has been a big success, both in terms of raising public awareness and in developing cutting-edge spatial strategies to combat climate change. At the same time, it has inspired similar initiatives across the United States, including *Changing Course* (2013), which challenged interdisciplinary design teams to develop strategies for the future of the Lower Mississippi River Delta, and ongoing projects in Miami and the San Francisco Bay Area. In each of these initiatives, adaptation to climate change is approached first and foremost as a *spatial* opportunity: by focusing on hybrid approaches that combine hard and soft engineering strategies, we can design landscapes that are dynamic and productive while cultivating new nature-culture relationships (Rojas et al 2015: 188).

The 1799 dike breach at Bemmel in the Netherlands by Christian Josi

Alongside developing new approaches to water management, there is a need to preserve cultural landscapes of traditional water management. As illustrated in this article, these landscapes have evolved over extended periods of time. They are key sources of knowledge concerning appropriate governance structures, social relations, spatial strategies and economic incentives essential to developing long-term sustainable water management. As pointed out by Kate Orff (2017): "Looking back reminds us that dramatic change in place, environment, and ecosystem is part of understanding current urban ecology, and critical in projecting forward newly modified cohabitats and communities." In the same way a site's history can inform future landscape proposals, historical water management approaches and techniques can guide us in developing new mechanisms moving forward. To do so we must develop solutions that neither over-romanticize the past nor simply revert to a 'technological fix' (Priscoli 1998). Instead, we should embrace the myriad of interactions among the human, non-human, and abiotic components of (urban) landscapes to develop a diversity of spatial models of water management.

ENDNOTES:

1 J. De Vries, "The Netherlands and the polder model: Questioning the polder model concept." *BMGN-the Low Countries Historical Review*, 129, no. 1, (2014), pp. 99 –111.

2 Dutch Water Authorities. 2015. *Water Governance: The Dutch Water Authority Model*. URL: http://www.dutchwaterauthorities.com/wp-content/uploads/2015/05/Water-Governance-The-Dutch-Water-Authority-Model1.pdf (accessed August 30, 2016)

3 A. Graber and R. Junge, "Aquaponic Systems: Nutrient Recycling from Fish Wastewater by Vegetable Production." *Desalination*, 246, (2009), pp. 147–156.

4 Carlo Giupponi and Animesh K. Gain, "Integrated Spatial Assessment of the Water, Energy and Food Dimensions of the Sustainable Development Goals." *Regional Environmental Change* (2016).

5 C. Gunn, "Acequias as Commons: Lessons for a Post-Capitalist World." *Review of Radical Political Economics*, 48: 1, (2016), pp. 81–89.

6 F. Hassan, Water History For Our Times: IHP Essays On Water History (United Nations Educational, Scientific and Cultural Organization, Paris: France), 2011.

7 M. E. Lewis and Craig L. Torbenson, "Cultural Antecedents of J. W. Powell's Arid Lands Report." *Journal of Geography,* 89, 2, (1990), pp. 74–80.

8 K. Lokman, "Dam[ned] landscapes: Envisioning fluid geographies." *Journal of Architectural Education* 70, 1, (2016), pp. 6–12.

9 K. Lokman, "Exploring a New Paradigm: Water management in Mexico City." *Topos: European Landscape Magazine*, 96, (2016), pp. 44–50.

10 K. Lokman, "Progressive Pragmatism: The Next Generation of Dutch Landscape Design Practices." *Proceedings of the Cracow Landscape Conference,* 2016, pp. 19–28. ISSN 2451-1692 http://www.clc.edu.pl/wp-content/uploads/2016/09/VOL_1_CLC2016.pdf.

11 Merlín-Uribe, Yair, et al. "Environmental and Socio-Economic Sustainability of Chinampas (Raised Beds) in Xochimilco, Mexico City." *International Journal of Agricultural Sustainability*, 11, 3, (2013), p. 216.

12 F. D. L. Nichols, et al. "Water management and political economy in formative period central Mexico." *Precolumbian Water Management: Ideology, Ritual, and Power.* (2006), pp. 51–66.

13 K. Orff, "Ideas." http://www.scapestudio.com/ideas/ (accessed February 8, 2017).

14 J. R. Parsons, "Political implications of prehispanic chinampas agriculture in the Valley of Mexico." *Land and politics in the Valley of Mexico. A two thousand year perspective.* (1991).

15 J. W. Powell, Report on the lands of the arid region of the United States: With a more detailed account of the lands of Utah with maps. (Government Printing Office: Washington, DC, 1878).

16 C. Rojas, B. De Meulder, and K. Shannon, "Water Urbanism in Bogota. Exploring the Potentials of an Interplay between Settlement Patterns and Water Management." *Habitat International,* 48, (2015), pp. 177–187.

17 N. Raheem, "A Common-Pool Resource Experiment in Acequia Communities." *International Journal Of The Commons,* 9, 1, (2015), pp. 306–321.

18 R. Roggema, Adaptation to Climate Change: A Spatial Challenge, Springer Science + Business Media, 2009: 59 –111.

19 C. Salewski, Dutch new worlds: Scenarios in physical planning and design in the Netherlands, 1970–2000 (Rotterdam: 010 Publishers, 2012).

20 W. T. Sanders, Robert S. Santley, and Jeffrey R. Parsons, The Basin of Mexico: The Ecological Processes in the Evolution of a Civilization (Academic Press: New York, 1979).

21 M. Santistevan, "Acequia Culture and the Regional Food System." https://coyotegulch.blog/2016/10/16/acequia-culture-and-the-regional-food-system-miguel-santistevan/ (accessed November 15, 2016).

22 JJ. Schmidt, and D. Shrubsole, "Modern Water Ethics: Implications for Shared Governance." *Environmental Values*, 22, 3, (2013), pp. 359–379.

23 P. B. Torres Lima, Canabal-Cristiani, and G. Burela-Rueda, "Urban Sustainable Agriculture: The Paradox of the Chinampa System in Mexico City." *Agriculture and Human Values*, 11, 1, (1994), pp. 37–46.

24 M. Van Tielhof, "Forced Solidarity: Maintenance of Coastal Defences Along the North Sea Coast in the Early Modern Period." *Environment and History*, 21, 3, (2015), pp. 319–350.

25 C.P. Veerman, "Foreword." In *Working together with water: A living land builds for its future.* Delta Committee: Hollandia Printing, 2008.

26 D. Worster, "A River Running West: Reflections on John Wesley Powell." *Journal of Cultural Geography*, 26, 2, (2009), pp. 113–126.

27 C. Zevenbergen, et al, "Taming Global Flood Disasters. Lessons Learned from Dutch Experience." *Natural Hazards*, 65, 3, (2013), pp. 1217–1225.

THE OYSTER BLOCKS PROJECT

SUBAQUEOUS INTERVENTIONS FOR NON-HUMANS

by MICHAEL LEIGHTON BEAMAN

Part .01

Subaqueous environments, those that are defined through their submersion under water, are inhuman environments, they do not afford human life. And while this alone might disqualify us from playing an active role in the formation and modification of these environments, it has not. Humans have affected these environments both intentionally and unintentionally for thousands of years. Most of our impact comes in the form of "non-design" interventions. This encompasses varying degrees of intentionality, but they lack a conscious design agenda. These interventions are predominantly the byproducts of multiple, dispersed domestic and industrial scale activities, or non-point origins. Agricultural runoff, waste disposal, leakages and other non-point source origins constitute a systemic distributed form of non-design authorship.

Though the manipulation of subaqueous environments may not have the practical or theoretical impact of land-based interventions, they are part of a larger anthropogenic remaking of the world. Reformation of the Earth's surface by collective human activity has accelerated exponentially since the Industrial Revolution. On average, humans displace twice the volume of Mount Fuji each year. This geological-scale adaptation of our environment has brought about the emergence of a new

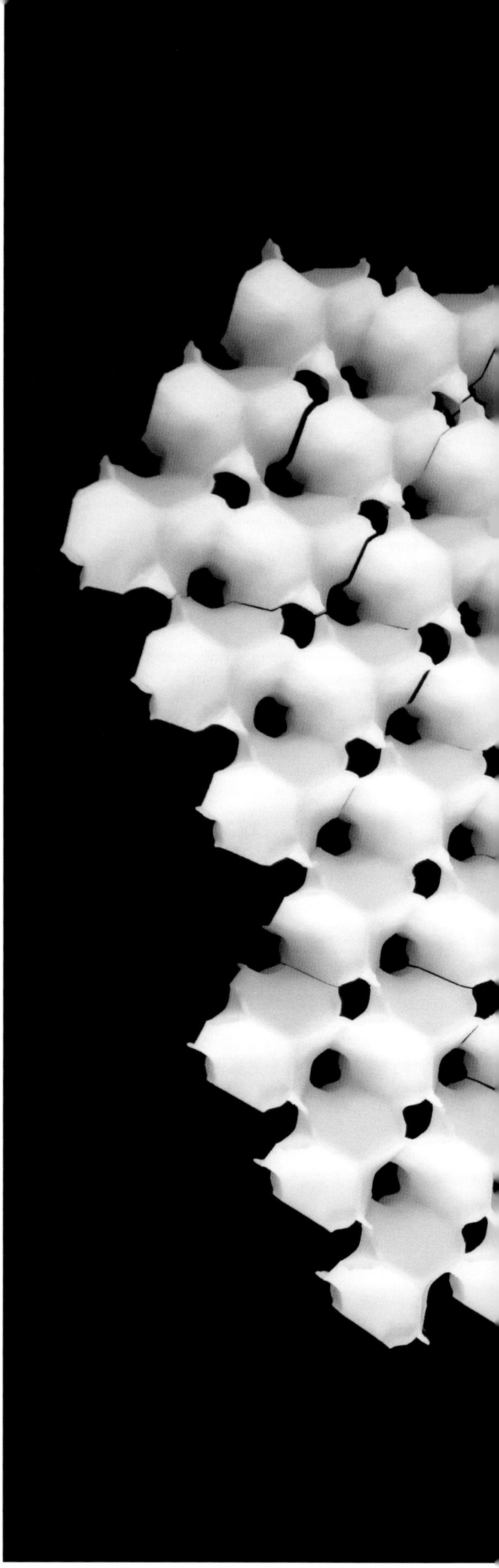

Oyster Block shown in a single layer configuration, 3D print in ABS plastic

geological era — the Anthropocene. Much of this activity occurs in what has been termed the Earth's event layer, which encompasses multiple environments.

For designers, with little exception, our practice is on dry land. However, from the dredging of the East River in New York, to the creation of artificial islands in the South China Sea, anthropogenic land formations are also designed to operate with and within water. Or, these Earth Surface transformations are simply the unintended products of fluvial processes operating on our interventions. These projects, whether because of their scale, complexity, or the specific ecological and hydrological concerns they embody, fall outside of the scope or interests of the design disciplines. As a result, they occupy a place somewhere between designed and non-designed environments.

Part .02

It is within the tradition of non-design interventions that the earliest artificial subaqueous environments are believed to have emerged, serendipitously through the artifacts of net-fishing practices. Fishing nets are an ensemble of materials and forms. Fibrous rope is tied together in regular intervals forming a flexible scaffold. Thinner cord is tied or woven into the spaces between in precisely spaced patterns tailored to the characteristics of local sealife. The addition of stone, metal, bone, and wooden hooks helped to ensure larger, stronger fish could not break free. Small nets could be thrown or swept through a water body by only a few people. Larger nets required coordination and time. Nets measuring over four-hundred feet in length and twenty feet in height were common in ancient Mediterranean and South American civilizations. But, these larger nets could not be easily moved through water and their yields became difficult to gather by hand. Eventually buoyant materials were attached to one edge, and at the other, heavy stones were tied, spreading the net vertically from the water's surface to the sea or river bed. Nets oriented in this fashion create a selectively porous wall. Fish are brought into the net by their own movements, tides and currents.

As nets grew in size, so too did intervals between harvests. When these larger nets, now full of fish, were pulled ashore or onboard boats, fishers simply cut away their ballast to manage the weight, depositing gagged stones on the seafloor. Over time, changes in the spatial dimensions of the seabed emerged. New topographies were generated, affecting the flow and trajectory of water. Cavities were created, protecting prey from predator. Mass was increased, mitigating shifts in temperature and changes in current. Surfaces accumulated, affording places for plants and animals to attach themselves and grow. What was merely debris generated changes in the composition of the ecosystem below the water's surface. Increases in seabed complexity correlated to increases in biomass; as a result, breeding increases, food sources increase, and fishing yields become more plentiful.

The use of discarded materials accounts for the majority of modified aquatic environments, either as an intentional act through scuttling ships or sinking used tires tied together in massive bundles; or as a byproduct of waste disposal practices — building and infrastructure construction or agriculture and aquaculture. In each case, the resulting reshaping of seabeds can be considered a reformation of the Earth's event layer, and a problem for designers to address. In the case of scuttled ships, their placement, orientation, and modification are considered, when repurposing them into environmental interventions. For tires and other modular waste materials, their pattern of aggregation and their collective formal qualities are considered. While manufactured systems are readily available, they form only a small fraction of these environments. More importantly, the degree to which they are non-design objects is of question.

Part .03

As more emphasis is placed on humanity's impact on the Earth's environments, and what might be called an acknowledgement and exploration of the ecological context of our activity, designers have become more involved in adaptive and interventional projects that are realized in larger, more interconnected ways. Increasingly, those projects are involving subaqueous environments and ecotones. These projects are expanding the notion of intervention and adaptation for designers to encompass water. The Oyster Blocks Project, which began as a collaboration between Betafield and Allied Concrete, was born from this approach to design intervention. Our collaborative goal was to investigate how manufactured elements, which play a role in these environments, might be reconsidered to be more specific in form, material, and construction; and more responsive in how they relate to their intended intervention and unintended effects.

The creation of artificial reefs is one of the earliest examples of a systematic and practiced subaqueous intervention. Modified aquatic environments are created for multiple reasons. One of the most widely used applications is to promote or mitigate the growth of sea life by creating environments calibrated to support specific species. Support can be generated by mitigating some condition already present, or amplifying an existing favorable condition. While these two functions are not mutually exclusive, they do help define the goals for intervention.

Artificial seabeds and reefs that are completely designed are typically done so through unitization and modularization to lower cost and facilitate in their placement and assembly. Whereas reused materials and

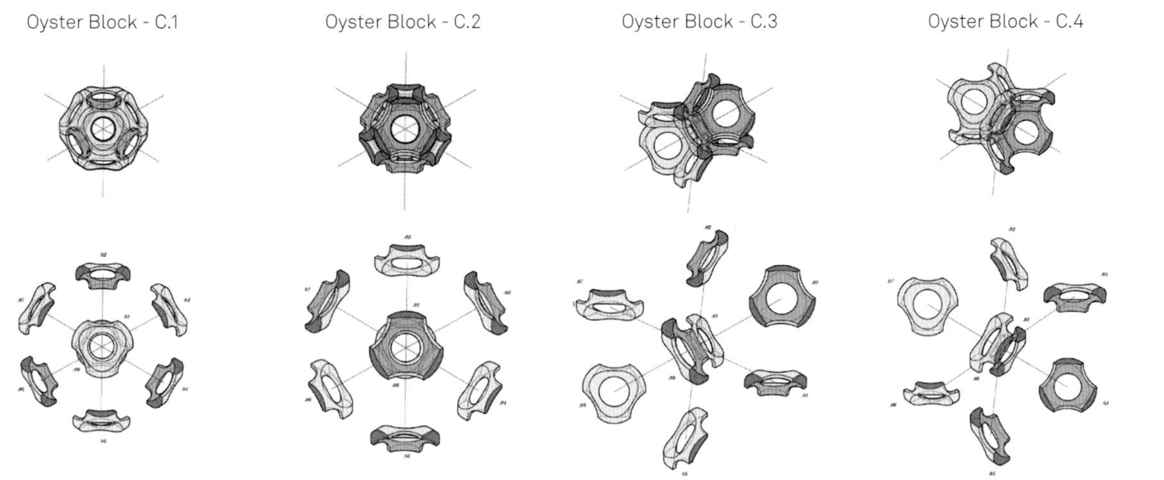

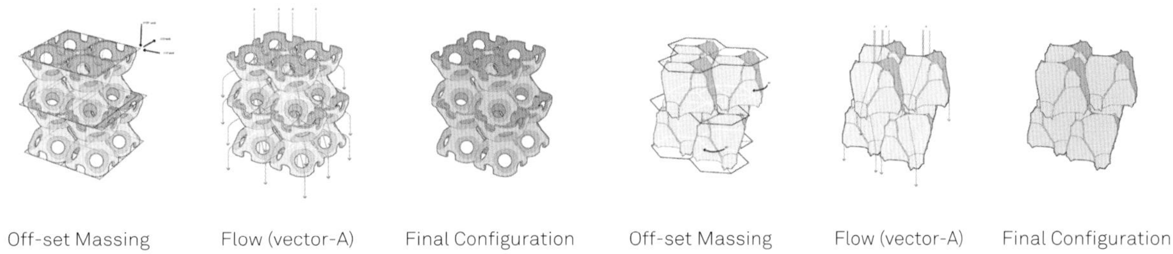

objects like ships and tires are only able to be modified, constructed units can be designed for specific performances or effects. They can be calibrated to effect specific environmental conditions such as water flow, and specific inhabitants such as fish, algae, or in the case of the Oyster Block Project, oysters.

We identified oyster farming in the Chesapeake Bay as a practice that had been affected by commercial fishing, industrial waste, transportation infrastructure, and changes in environmental conditions; and proposed this as the context in which to work. The project, though initially just focused on research, presented an opportunity to examine the larger issues of anthropogenic landformation practices as a problem within three of our core areas of interest: materials research, design technology, and environmental impact.

Part .04

The unitized, modular approach was one we were interested in building upon. This approach has been used in Japan as far back as the mid-eighteenth century and throughout the world since the early twentieth century. The adoption of manufactured reef units was spurred in large part by the accessibility of mass production techniques and advances in material science. The digital modeling, simulation and manufacturing advances, which are folded into mass production today, expose a way to expand the correlation between unique environmental conditions and artificial reef unit design. We began by addressing the issues of form, material, and construction in a more relational way, in which performance criteria could be modulated by morphology, composition, and assembly. Through Morphology, we examined the unit and aggregate form, Compositon, the environmental effects of each unit's material makeup, and Assembly, the organizational, structural and product of each unit - with all three considerations impacting the final design. The project spawned five typologies: Oyster Blocks A-E. Each foregrounded one of the three considerations over others, while addressing the central function of creating artificial reefs for oyster farming.

Block form or unit morphology, and aggregate pattern or collective morphology, are closely linked. While all unitized reef modules accumulate, the question for us was how we could create effects present in the aggregate that were not present in the unit. Since the collective, not the individual, creates the performative effect, we began by examining how a collective morphology could guide design. These effects generated a mitigation or exaggeration of local aquatic conditions and influenced the orientation or directionality of unit aggregation. Oyster Block series A for example was concerned with creating a thickened and articulated surface, whereas series B and C examined multi-directional and rotational aggregations. Likewise, orientation

TOP
Alternative part-to-unit configurations
BOTTOM
Unit alignment strategy & water flow diagram

and directionality of effect was also a consideration. Oyster Block series E allowed for deviated, but relatively clear paths for water flow along one vector, while constraining movement in others, creating various degrees of resistance through changes in direction. Directional changes generated occluded or sheltered surfaces that promote biodiversity.

Material composition has both global and local effects. These can include: compressive and tensile strength, mechanical and chemical erosion resistance, density, porosity, texture, and color. These material effects impact both design considerations and performance considerations. For instance, smooth surface textures reduce friction and resist mechanical erosion from moving water. Rougher textures allow for the attachment of mollusk and barnacle stalks. Some materials resist chemical erosion from mineral deposits by packing tighter, while others provide a better substrate for shell growth. The three main components of each unit are cement, aggregate, and additives. Within these three, there are variations in chemical composition and physical characteristics, such as particle size. Both chemical and physical recipes were tested with Allied Concrete, each tuned to the chemical makeup of different areas of the Chesapeake Bay, in order to promote more habitable conditions for local oyster species.

Assemblies were examined in multiple scales and stages of production. The first scale we considered was that of the unit itself. Working exclusively with cast materials meant that each unit had to be described geometrically through multi-part, reusable molds. While the constraints of reusable molds limit certain geometric complexity, it also allowed for variation in the unit itself, by conceiving of the mold as a design problem itself. We began by understanding that like the units, molds are comprised of parts, which can be rearranged and reassembled to produce different final unit configurations. As was the case with Oyster Blocks C.1, C.2, C.3 and C.4, mold parts could be reconfigured to create more open or enclosed units. Likewise, duplicate mold parts can be used to created three-dimensionally variable units, in the case of Oyster Block series E, which is created by six identical interlocking mold parts. The second scale of assembly is how each unit, once cast, is able to lock in place with other units to form an aggregation pattern. In both the C and E series, units nested through interlocking features, created to ensure alignment during unit placement in a site, so that voids and surfaces were continuous throughout the aggregation to produce predictable effects.

Part .05

These three considerations allowed the project to be developed as a series. The series framework allowed us to take a parametric approach to integrating the three main criteria above. That is to say, that not only could geometric definitions be generated by the relationships, as is the case in parametricism, but that all three characteristic were explored as interconnected contingencies within the design process. The Oyster Block, as a series of design solutions, explored through a conceptually parametric design process, also allowed us to foreground specific characteristics with the knowledge that others would not be ignored, only hierarchically displaced. Variability within a typology or variations between typologies could then be more tightly explored and rigorously tested.

Working primarily in a digital environment meant that aggregation patterns of hundreds of units could be tested using flow simulations. These were typically

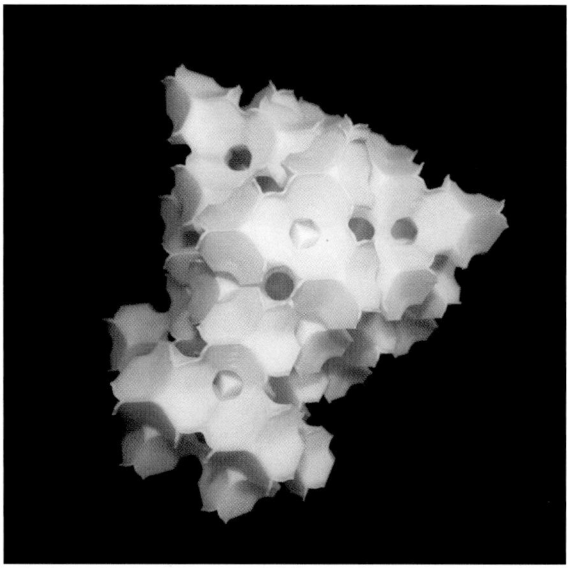

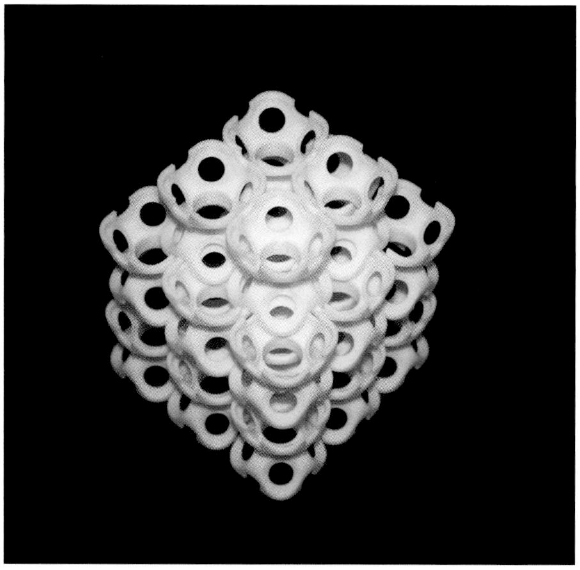

Oyster Block shown in two packing configurations, 3D print in ABS plastic

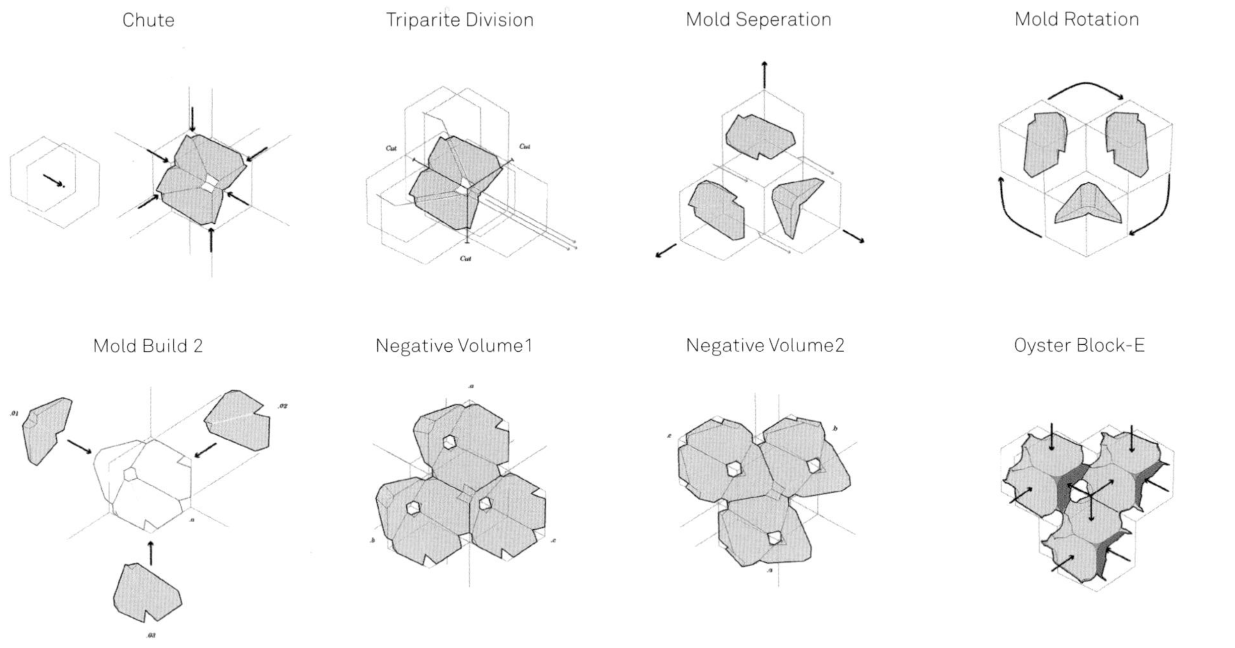

done using discrete particle tests, but could easily be extended to more computationally expensive simulations. The monolithic nature of the Oyster Block units lent themselves to exploration in physical simulations through 3-D printing. This mid-step before prototyping provided us a chance to test aggregation tolerances, water flow impact, and an opportunity for experimentation. This promoted the development of project insights difficult to realize in a digital environment. Alternative packing or stacking geometries could be tested as well as aggregation misalignments and unit stabilities. 3-D printing also provided a way to test molding strategies, using the same methodologies. The research, while not realized as fully manufactured units, is part of a larger research path Beta-field has pursued over the last few years. This path closely examines designed landformations and their impact on the built environment.

Our own involvement with understanding how designers might intervene in the course of anthropogenic landformation are either analytical in nature or carry with them all the considerations of human activity, desire, and sensibility. The Oyster Block project builds on our research into establishing practices, which bridge computational design and simulation methodologies with data-driven form generation, human-nonhuman collaborative production techniques, and materials research. The project has been instrumental in expanding this approach to other more traditional architecture and landscape architecture projects, focusing on the question of designing for non-humans in a way that recognizes our role as designers in reshaping our environment in an explicit and novel way.

ENDNOTES:

1 Diana Agrest outlines the term "non-design" as being objects that have purpose and intention, but that are not the product of a design process.

Diana Agrest, "Design Versus Non-Design," in *Oppositions*, No.6 (Fall 1976), pp 45–67.

2 National Oceanic and Atmospheric Association. "Ocean Pollution" http://www.noaa.gov/resource-collections/ocean-pollution. Accessed Jan 12, 2017.

3 Bruce H. Wilkenson, "Humans as Geologic Agents: A Deep-time Perspective," *Geology.* 33, 3, (2003). p. 161–164.

4 Paul Crutzen, "Geology of Mankind," *Nature*, 415, (2002).

5 Richard Christian, Frank Steimle and Richard Stone, "Evolution of Marine Artificial Reef Development — A philosophical Review of Management," *Gulf of Mexico Science*. 16 (1), (1998).

Water chute geometry and mold reconfiguration

The hammam, a public place next to the mosque

THE HAMMAM OF ERBIL CITADEL

A CONFLUENCE OF PAST, PRESENT, AND FUTURE

by AHMED ABBAS & KAREN LENS

Iraq has a very old and rich cultural history. Due to the wars in the region, much of this history has been lost. This applies particularly to the citadel in the city of Erbil, protected as one of world's oldest, permanently inhabited urban settlements. Over more than 6.000 years this UNESCO World Heritage Site has been, without interruption, a military, religious and cultural stronghold in the Kurdish steppe of northern Iraq. The fortress is situated on top of an artificial, elliptical archaeological mound, 32 meters above the flat city and its surroundings.
Its dense urban fabric consists mainly of brick houses with traditional courtyards. Scattered among the town's complex fabric are a prison, seven historic graves, a Koran school, three gates and several squares They are revealed as you stroll through the narrow streets, evidence of the citadel as a self-sustaining system with a military, political, legal, economic and housing infrastructure. The narrow streets of this age-old labyrinth provide continuous shade, induce pleasant breezes during the hot summers and give shelter during cold, hard winters.
In the center of the citadel was a public bath, a Hammam, built next to one of the city's three mosques. Founded in 1775 by Qassim Agha Abdullah, who was inspired by traditional Islamic principles, this public bath was traditionally constructed with close links to its urban context and in accordance with socio-cultural norms of the society within which it operated. (A.Al-Haidari, (2014)). The well, a basic component, is still present today, but no longer in use. It provided water for drinking, cleaning and bathing in a common facility of purity, the Hammam.

Recently, an ambitious project has commenced to conserve and revitalize Erbil Citadel. This project has two main objectives. The first

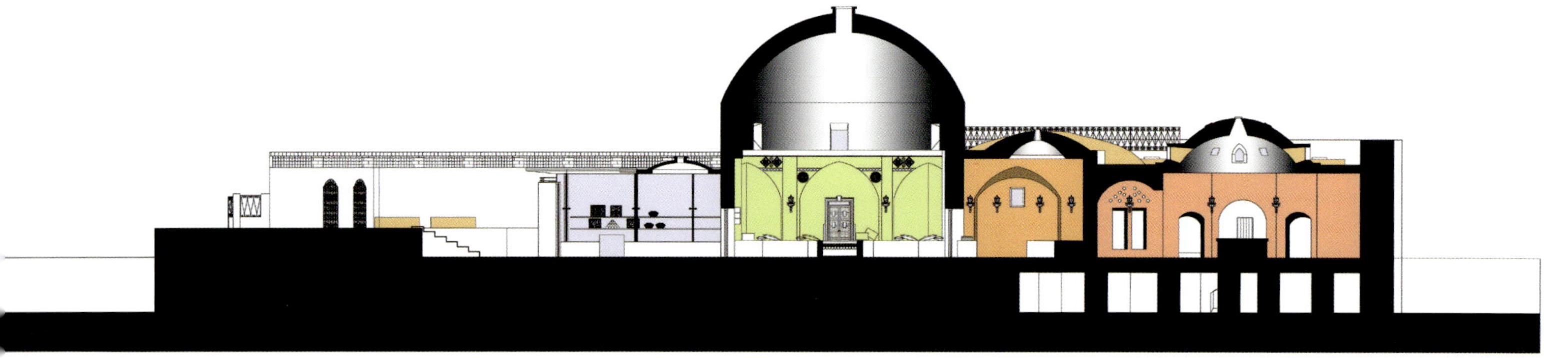

comprises physical conservation procedures to preserve and improve the architectural, physical and structural quality of the citadel buildings. The second entails adaptive reuse procedures to deal with the preserved buildings. With the aim of bringing the citadel back to life as a centre for culture, recreation and tourism, adaptive reuse has been adopted as the core strategy for a culture-driven revitalization. Within this context, this paper intends to contribute to the revitalization of the citadel by focusing on an important element of its urban fabric, the public bath (Hammam). In accordance with the guidelines of the Burra Charter, our project aims to protect a significant and valuable part of this cultural world heritage site (Burra Charter, (1999)) through our design of the Hammam as a renovated bathhouse instead of as a museum as previously proposed[1] (Al Yaqoobi, (2014)). Once again water will connect the citizens of Erbil and its visitors as modern techniques and designs are combined with ancient traditions and architecture. This proposed adaptive reuse process not only represents a source of inspiration for revitalizing the entire citadel, but through water it also constitutes a catalyst for its redevelopment (Yaraly.B. (2001)).

The significance of the Citadel hammam has its origin in the various functions and purposes, which are accommodated historically on its grounds. As a place of entertainment, this bathhouse, just like the fountains in the courtyards of the townhouses, acted as a source of cooling and relaxation (Al Yaqoobi. (2012)). In addition, the hammam complex was a place of hygiene as it was built originally to support the Citadel's citizens physically as well as spiritually. The Hammam's spatial organization incorporated a purifying religious force for both mind and body. As one of its many functions, the Hamman stimulated the senses. The further one entered the successive areas, the more the world quieted; filtered light is reflected, complex scents of herbs and soap are identified, hot air envelops the visitor, and sins are washed away. The purifying effect of the hammam was not only physical but also held a deeper and religious significance: a cleansing of the mind by scrubbing the sins of the body. (A.Al-Haidari. (2014))

From its inception, the hammam was also a place of social significance. The water brought together citizens without distinction, even the most isolated women. Public bathing and traditional massage formed an important weekly or even daily ritual. As such this facility had a strong social function. Waiting times for bathing created social opportunities. The hammam became a meeting place for both men and women. Visitors exchanged news items; dissatisfaction and political unrest in the city are discussed among all sections of the population. The bathhouse was even the only social gathering place for isolated Muslim women, who lived permanently in the seclusion of their houses. It was the single place where they could come into contact with other women outside their immediate family circle.

Islamic bathhouses often function as a public forum. Hammams were used for all kinds of ceremonies of great significance in the lives of ordinary Muslims. People usually gathered here during the day, but they also organized events or even prayer services in this public space next to the mosque. The hammam was the location to assess the physical qualities of a prospective bride by their new female relatives. When a potential daughter-in-law had been selected, she was invited to visit the hammam with her family-to-be. This 'test' was critical for the marriage to be concluded. This was followed later by an inspection of men in the bathhouse in preparation for their wedding. (Derbandi,N,A., (2008)) One of the most important ceremonies at the hammam took place when a baby was 40 days old. The child was brought to the bathhouse to undergo a traditional washing ritual in order to become a member of society. Different festivals took place with music, drinks and food, such as henna, farewell and birthday parties and so on. People who converted to Islam were taken to the bathhouse. And finally, residents came to bathe when they experienced difficult or decisive moments in their lives. When war or disease hit the country, people tried to find peace in the comfortable hot steam of the hammam.

The functions of Hammam previously mentioned are supported and, in fact, accomplished overall by its spatial organization: the Camekan, the Westani, and

Section of proposed scheme

the Harret. A normal bathhouse consists of three major components that are interconnected. The first room a bather passes is the 'Alberani', which is the cool or lukewarm space combined with the 'Camekan' or the entrance area. This area serves as a social meeting point and dressing area where a visitor drapes a pestemal or a traditional flat-woven Turkish towel around the waist over a cloth of silk or cotton. The next space, which is called the 'Westani' or 'the middle', is a warmer room. The middle room may not be of high importance to visitors, but, in fact, it is most essential to the hammam. Without the 'Westani' the bathhouse misses a certain rhythm necessary for its proper functioning. The human body can cope with very high and low temperatures as long it has the time to adapt or to recover. When going from a dark to a light place or the other way round, one's eyes need time to acclimate. The long corridor of this middle room serves as a place for adjusting to the differences in both temperature and lighting. For this reason, the Westani is irreplaceable in the hammam's process. After having adjusted gently to the heat and light in the lukewarm middle room on one of the massage beds, one can spend time in the hottest space of the facility, the 'Harret'. This space is permanently filled with steam, the place where people wash and cleanse themselves, not only physically but also mentally. In the ceiling of this room there usually is a dome with small windows to let in filtered natural light into an otherwise dark space below. In the middle of this space there is a platform with a marble surface, referred to as the belly or sweat stone used for the traditional rough massages. In the corners of this space are water fountains or showers for washing and rinsing of the body and hair. Large hammams have two of these areas, one for men and one for women, whereas the smaller hammans use a strict separate time schedule for each sex. (E.Resul. ((2005)) After the thorough treatment, a bather walks slowly back to the Alberan, where one can dry while drinking a cup of tea or milk.

In order to be an integral part of the Erbil Citadel Revitalization Project, our project, in conformity with the Burra Charter guidelines, proposes a policy for the Hammam that identifies a use or combination of uses to retain the cultural significance of the place and specifically its social significance. The basic idea of the design is to reshape the building and to make it operational as a hammam once more. As a principal criterion for achieving this objective, the proposed interventions on any level and any scale should be minimal. A restored use of the place, with minimal changes to the principal physical structure and uses, should respect associations and meanings and, where appropriate, should provide for the continuation of practices which contribute to the local culture. As respect for culture and existing valuable elements must be the most natural approach in this process (Plevoets, B., & Van Cleempoel, K. (2013)), it is crucial to use material from the area itself. Such an approach keeps the design close

Built in seats inside the hammam

to the culture of the place and preserves the identity of the historical city and hammam as a typical Islamic construction. The bathhouse functioning once again as a real hammam instead of the proposed new use of museum enables a first-hand experience of the cultural past. At the original open courtyard of this public space, we placed traditional trees, benches and a small water source to invite people to come and gather as they used to. Through maintaining the existing conditions and spaces, the infrastructure will welcome the visitor through a confluence of past, present and future.

The exterior of the hammam will maintain its current and traditional appearance through restoration, whereas the inside will be almost entirely recoated, using typical Iraqi and Kurdish materials and modern techniques. The new design maintains the apertures and skylights that allow natural lighting from above. Spatial interventions into the interior include the introduction of

new seating in the changing room, lockers, a footbath, a division of the harret to create two contemporary saunas, updated toilets and a small shop.

Interventions are also made to update the water heating system. Historically, heat was produced by burning manure and waste, which was subsequently transported under the building through tunnels based on the system of the Roman thermal baths. The biggest fire burned under the hot belly stone or the center of the traditional bathhouse. Instead, we introduce environmentally respectful methods for heating the water through the use of the sun and the wind, combined with a minimum of electricity and gas. The tunnels remain the same although they now contain a modern ventilation system. The thickness of brick walls and other passive cooling techniques, such as semi-basements like the tunnels and small windows, offer added advantages. The old and the new strengthen each other.

A proper system like the hammam of Erbil does not require essential changes in order to revive on an architectural and social level. Its manual is easy to read when one feels the original atmosphere of the various rooms. In the restored monument, the historical operation remains identifiable to the local residents to whom the site has special associations and meanings. Like the Burra Charter predetermines, the people of Erbil are invited to assume the essential social, spiritual or other cultural responsibilities of the place by integrating it back into their lives. However, the minimal changes provide the opportunity for visitors of this heritage to experience foreign cultural values in a climate of co-existence without the loss of the original, social and spiritual characteristics.

This adaptive reuse proposal of minimal intervention reveals a central thread, which can be translated to similar heritage sites. Muslim communities from North Africa, the Middle East to Central Asia share the same architectural principles. Their constructions all try to secure functional necessities through standards and systems at home, at work and in public spaces. In spite of these similarities, local surroundings, culture and art have a physical impact on all constructions. Typical materials, space formations, architectural elements, decorations and inscriptions create clear distinctions. Furthermore, public and religious sites, including hammams, received additional attention during their building process because they visualised the nature and spirit of its users. The bathhouses combined daily and sacred life by providing water to support body and soul. Therefore, remaining hammams should be regarded as gems of cultural heritage that reconnect people to their past but also to their future. The cultural and artistic elements have a better chance of being maintained for following generations if they remain in use. The water in the hammam becomes a catalyst for rebuilding both the heritage and the community in the citadel of Erbil without any loss of identity. A judicious, adaptive reuse is the only method for maintaining specific, vulnerable sites within society in order to preserve contemporary rituals.

ENDNOTES:

1 From an interview with Mr. Al Yaqoobi Dara (Head of High Commission for Erbil Citadel Revitalization) in 4/17/2014

(re)MADE BY WATER

OBSOLESCENCE, URBAN NOMADISM AND THE NEW WORLD MALL, BANGKOK

by GREGORY MARINIC

In 1997, an extension to the New World Mall in central Bangkok was ordered to cease operations by the Supreme Court of Thailand due to an unlawful addition. To conform with the court order, owners responded by demolishing the top stories of the annex and abandoning it. The deserted structure attracted vandals who set fires that further exposed the interior to the elements. Monsoon rains slowly flooded the ground floor into a pool of water which came to host tropical fish and aquatic plants. Over the next twenty years, this 'dead' mall incrementally evolved into an ecology connecting the local community to the global backpacker circuit. Here, water radically remade a conventional space of consumption into a place of rogue tourism.

This essay engages my ongoing research of retail architecture and urban obsolescence. It examines how corrupt development practices and partial destruction transformed an ordinary shopping mall into an extraordinary aquatic landscape. This essay acknowledges informal methods of adaptive reuse mobilized by ecology, people, and everyday actions. It begins with an overview of the historical interface of water and architecture in Southeast Asia to provide context for this blended building-landscape. The writing aims to construct a broader narrative surrounding the New World Mall in relation to the spatial theories of Walter

The New World Mall, Bangkok

Benjamin, Guy Debord, Henri Lefebvre, and Anthony Vidler, as well as practices of urban nomadism across time and cultures. Further, the essay frames a socio-cultural perspective on retail architecture unintentionally remade with water, adapted through everyday practices and rediscovered by global wanderers—a new flâneurie.

Water and Architecture in Southeast Asia: A Brief Overview

Across the geographically and culturally diverse region of Southeast Asia, water has historically served as a primary feature in both sacred architecture and urbanism. Beginning in the third century BCE, the Hindu and Buddhist religions expanded from India into the Indochinese Peninsula via sea trading and overland migration. At the beginning of the Common Era, Indian merchants brought Hindu Brahmins and Buddhist priests to settle in the region.[1] By the end of the first century, many of the kingdoms of Southeast Asia had adopted Hindu and Buddhist traditions suited to their needs. Since then, both faiths have imparted significant influences on social organization, literature, art, architecture, and urbanism in the region.

Water is revered in the Hindu and Buddhist traditions for its purity, cleansing powers, and spiritual properties. Ancient Sanskrit texts advise that temple sites should include water features that support the growth of lotus, water fowl, song birds, and fish.[2] Vedic scripture states that such characteristics were meant to engender nirvana and the idyllic realm of deities. As such, the holiest Hindu pilgrimage sites are located along rivers and lakes, while temple compounds in urban environments incorporate constructed pools used for ritual bathing. Similarly, Buddhism employs water as reflecting pools, ponds, and lakes in the landscape design of temple complexes. Monumental Hindu temples to Vishnu and Shiva, for example, were built during the ancient Khmer empire along major bodies of water.[3] Among the most impressive, Angkor Wat was conceived during the twelfth century as a Hindu temple and later converted to Buddhist use. Surrounded by ramparts and a moat teeming with lotus and koi, it demonstrates a strong connection between sacred architecture and water, as well as a spatial fluidity linking the Buddhist and Hindu traditions. Today, the nations of Southeast Asia share water aesthetics informed by these hybrid influences.

In contemporary Bangkok, water is an omnipresent and atmospheric condition in the city. Known as 'The Venice of the East', the Thai capital was historically defined by a vast network of khlongs (canals) which connected the Chao Phraya River with districts and neighborhoods throughout the urban core. From the fourteenth through the nineteenth centuries, floating markets served as nodes which spawned the growth of mercantile, social, and cultural activities.[4] Floating markets allowed farmers and merchants to sells agricultural products, prepared foods, textiles, and other goods directly from their boats. By the twentieth century, however, road and rail networks began to supplant many of the khlongs, while at the same time, others were eliminated due to public health and sanitation concerns.[5] Today, the Chao Phraya River continues to serve as a primary commuter artery in Bangkok, while floating markets remain active in Wat Sai, Taling Chan, and Khlong Lat Mayom.

Theoretical Framework: Consumption, Obsolescence, and Flâneurie

It is important to situate the lifecycle of the New World Mall within a broader social, historical, and theoretical context. Since the early twentieth century, theorists have routinely critiqued the impact of capitalism on buildings and urban space. It is widely acknowledged that the consumptive origins of contemporary society may be traced to the whims, desires, and projections of the nineteenth century. As evidenced by the twentieth century transition from arcades to department stores, and later, by twenty-first century shifts from a physical world of shopping malls to the virtual world of internet commerce, retail environments have become increasingly obsolete. Continual changes in production, communication, and connectivity have radically transformed the rules of retail, as well as the future of retail building typologies around the world.

Over the course of the twentieth century, theorists Walter Benjamin, Guy Debord, Henri Lefebvre, and Anthony Vidler analyzed the influence of consumption on urbanism and architectural form. Beginning in the 1930s, Walter Benjamin studied the Parisian arcades to discern the social, architectural, and phenomenological conditions of a declining nineteenth century retail typology. In his seminal work, "The Arcades Project", Benjamin viewed the arcades as a visual device, or space frame, that provided the bourgeoisie a curated view on life. Within the confines of these interior worlds, expectations changed and contemporary consumerism emerged.[6] Benjamin alluded to dreams and fantasies—of the simultaneity of the literal world contrasting with an alternative, controlled, and sublime one existing within the sky-lit arcades. Alongside retailing, the Parisian arcades supported an underworld of illegal and illicit activities. Vices such as gambling and prostitution were beyond direct police jurisdiction, spawning a broader bohemian culture of transients, artists, and gays which challenged racial, ethnic, and socio-economic boundaries.

Benjamin's research on the Parisian arcades was influenced by the poetry of Charles Baudelaire and his characterization of the nineteenth century flâneur as a gentleman stroller of the streets.[7] For Baudelaire, the flâneur represented the sophisticated urban aficionado who was recast by Benjamin as both a dandy and connoisseur of the modern metropolitan experience. The flâneur was an object of significant scholarly analysis, critique, and understanding of twentieth century urbanity and social conditions. Flâneurs revealed class tensions and gender divisions of the nineteenth century city, while their behaviors shed light on to a broader sense of alienation with modernity, mass production, consumer culture, and societal expectations. In this sense, the flâneurie were not simply limited to the physical act of strolling in the Baudelairian sense, but also implied an enlightened way of thinking, living, and navigating the world.

Representing a hybrid social type, flâneurs were at once a product of the bourgeoisie and the bohème.[8] Benjamin framed the flâneur as the definitive figure of the modern era, however, it was the habitats of the male flaneur in which he was primarily interested. As an urban stroller and loiterer, perhaps without an ostensible purpose, the flâneur was intuitively invested in the history of the city. In search of the sublime, delightful, or erotic — he wandered the boulevards, parks, cafés, and arcades. The urban forms which gave rise to flâneur culture simultaneously conveyed both aspirational largesse and zones of alienation in the city.[9] Although the flâneurs met their demise with the triumph of consumerism, other forms of this socio-cultural phenomenon reemerged in the contemporary era. Today, urban nomads and global backpackers seek out authentic experiences in a similar manner to the flâneurs, yet on a transcontinental scale.

Urban Nomadism and Everyday Forgotten Space in Bangkok

The impact of human activities on cities and within

buildings makes the study of the everyday a compelling filter for designers. Unlike the formalized rituals of design, everyday manipulations are anonymous, layered, and unstructured actions likened to social needs and cultural traditions.[10] Independent from the formal hand of professional architects and designers, everyday manipulations — ranging from post-occupancy changes to ground-up adaptations — significantly shape the functional, aesthetic, and qualitative aspects of the built environment. Henri Lefebvre acknowledged the everyday impact of production, consumption, and multiplicity of authorship in the built environment. He asserted that cities, buildings, and interiors are hybrid productions authored not only by designers, but also through cultural traditions, social practices, and autonomous interventions.[11] As a Marxist theorist who was critical of economic structuralism, Lefebvre proposed that the everyday manipulation of space is fundamental to the growth of society and the shape of the city.[12] He posits a theoretical perspective that distrusts the heroic, formal, and fashionable, while condemning design practices that operate as agents of commodification. Reframing the design of the built environment with the inverse — the everyday impact of people reshaping space — he celebrates the ordinary actions that cities, buildings, and interiors receive apart from the top-down hand of designers. Lefebvre fixes his gaze on the lives of designed spaces well beyond the moment of their completion.

The abandoned mall filled with rainwater

In 1956, Guy Debord defined the term dérive as "a mode of experimental behavior linked to the conditions of urban society, a technique of rapid passage through varied ambiances." As a founding member of Situationist International, he contributed to shaping a mid-twentieth century discourse of urban drifting which embraced playfulness, constructive exploration, and awareness of psycho-geographical effects.[13] The dérive, a form of urban exploration, demonstrated a significantly alternative engagement with the city than the typical journey or stroll. More akin to the studied encounters of the flâneur, Debord and his Situationist collaborators sought to identify fissures in cities, distinct neighborhoods with no correlation to administrative boundaries, the role of urban micro-climates, and the character of places of attraction. As political revolutionaries and provocateurs of the 1960s counterculture, Situationists proposed a different way to read, analyze, and critique cities. They acknowledged the inherent value of marginalized urban spaces.

The counterculture of the 1960s emerged from the earlier Beat Generation as an anti-establishment social, cultural, and political movement. Its origins may be traced to European bohemianism and a rising awareness of Eastern religions and spirituality.[14] The "hippie" subculture found significant inspiration in non-western cultural traditions and was defined by an ethos of communal living, creative experimentation, ecological balance, and recreational drug usage. From the mid-1960s to the late 1970s, young people from North America and Europe incrementally forged an overland route to the East.[15] The "hippie trail" began in London, moved across continental Europe to Istanbul, and then traversed the Middle East and Indian subcontinent to Bangkok. This alternative, modest, and interactive form of tourism contrasted sharply with the bourgeois tastes of the jet set. The trail was defined by hostels, cafés, and shops that catered almost exclusively to Westerners as they journeyed both east and west.[16] Much like the nineteenth century flâneurs, these global wanderers sought out the sublime, delightful, and erotic by wandering the bazaars, temples, and markets of the East. Although the hippie trail ended by the late 1970s due to political upheaval in Iran and Afghanistan, its influence on contemporary backpacker culture endures along fragments of the original route.

As Westerners migrated east in pursuit of authentic experiences, the East was developmentally moving west in pursuit of urban modernization and economic expansion. By the early 1970s, a first generation of shopping malls were built in the national capitals of Southeast Asia, joining a retail landscape historically

defined by shophouses, open-air markets, hawker stalls, and department stores.[17] Traditional commercial types were violently displaced in a wave of urban renewal that forged broader streets, infrastructure, and office towers.[18] Retail activities were increasingly relocated and encapsulated within the earliest shopping malls. In 1973, Siam Center opened as the first climate-controlled mall in Bangkok achieving an international standard. Housing sixty shops and the offices of Pan American World Airways and Chase Manhattan Bank, it set a new precedent for retailing in the central business district.[19] By the early 1980s, enclosed shopping malls became increasingly common place, and later, over-building throughout the 1990s and early 2000s resulted in notable levels of underuse and abandonment.[20] Today, many of the oldest malls in Bangkok have migrated toward remarkably alternative uses.

Located in the Bang Lamphu district, the New World Mall opened in 1982 during the second wave of shopping mall construction. In 1997, a court order filed by the Bangkok Metropolitan Administration claimed that an extension to the mall had been built seven stories taller than approved.[21] In response to the court order, the owners of New World Mall haphazardly demolished its outlawed floors. The compromised structure attracted arsonists who attempted to burn it down in retaliation for being taller than the Grand Palace.[22] Meanwhile, the abandoned mall filled with rainwater, while the exposed floor plates slowly came to host vegetation. Since its closure, litigation between municipal authorities and the owners has focused on who should fully demolish the building or rebuild its roof.

In 2003, residents of the surrounding community released koi, tilapia, and catfish into the waterscape to combat the mosquito nuisance.[23] Locals introduced tourists to the space and began selling food to feed the fish.[24] In 2013, 30-year old American backpacker Jesse Rockwell stumbled across New World Mall and wrote a blog post to document his visit.[25] By mid-2014, Rockwell's blog was discovered by a popular website, The Verge, and interest in the New World Mall went viral.[26] Cyberspace has transformed the mall into a popular stop along the global backpacker trail, while proximity to the Khao San Road hostel district made it accessible to the masses. With increased foot traffic, the narrow alleys surrounding New World Mall spawned mom-and-pop shops and cafés serving a rogue tourist industry.

The mall as an aquatic landscape

In an ironic twist of fate — embedded within a city known for its floating markets — the New World Mall represents a radical inversion of retail and water. Blending the vastness of a temple complex with the spatial ambiance of walled aquatic gardens, New World Mall has recast the sacred relationship of water, koi, building, and landscape. Although this unplanned "aquarium" remains extremely popular with tourists, as well as economically beneficial to its surrounding community, municipal authorities view it as a public hazard. In January 2015, fishermen were dispatched by municipal authorities to net the fish for transport to the Thai Department of Fisheries and various bodies of water throughout Thailand.[27] Although entering the former shopping mall remains illegal, urban explorers continue to find their way into the condemned structure. Haunted by a recent past much like the dying arcades of Benjamin's Paris in the 1930s, the New World Mall rests in limbo between politics and the people awaiting an uncertain future.

Reflection

Urban theorist Anthony Vidler uses the term "uncanny" as a metaphor for unplanned influences. In his book, *The Architectural Uncanny*, he analyzes obsolescence in everyday buildings of the recent past — abandoned shopping malls — as the after effects of consumerism, corporate disinvestment, and post-industrial culture.[28] Like Benjamin's analysis of the arcades, Vidler considers the trajectory of buildings that lose their purposefulness and fade to host alternative uses. He proposes a future vision of retail environments built upon their advancing obsolescence. In a similar manner, the New World Mall has been detached from its intended uses and appropriated by others. It documents a recent past embedded within the dense urban fabric of central Bangkok. As both a public interior and an aquatic landscape, New World Mall exists along the undefined margins of the built environment by means of incremental, parasitic, and illegal actions. Furthermore, the appropriated mall demonstrates subtle similarities with the walled, water-oriented sacred spaces common to both the Hindu and Buddhist traditions of Southeast Asia. Here, water became a force of spatial appropriation and cultural expression that motivated communal responses. Water represents an informal occupancy that has reshaped the larger built environment, from the inside-out, via natural processes of adaptive reuse. Water became a catalyst for human actions ranging from community mobilization to mercantilism and rogue tourism.

Through an uncommon convergence of circumstances, New World Mall demonstrates how ecology and people transformed an obsolete shopping mall into a place of delight for the twenty-first century flâneurie. Intentionally destabilized by government-sanctioned demolition, this structure also offers a perspective on the transformative forces impacting retail infrastructure worldwide. While internet-based retail threatens the worldwide viability of sustaining overbuilt physical environments, aging shopping malls also fall prey to shifting urban-suburban redevelopment strategies. In the case of New World Mall, the marriage of physical destruction and water allowed an interior urban space to organically grow within the ruins of a failed space of consumption.

From a design perspective, the temporal nature of retail buildings coupled with shifting socio-economic conditions fuels a vast interior territory of worldwide obsolescence, abandonment, and potential for regeneration. Viewed through the structuralist theoretical perspective of Lefebvre, this de-programmed mall has never been empty — it resonates with subtle traces of the past, fosters social interaction, and draws tourism with links to the Situationist dérive. Today, however, the mall exists within a markedly different era defined by the immediacy of social media connectivity to the masses.

It is critical that architects, landscape architects, and interior designers, as makers of the built environment, intentionally anticipate non-conforming future uses in their work. As evidenced here, disruptive and destructive forces can informally reactivate underused buildings and infrastructures. Design scholars and educators should critically engage the ways in which informal occupancies spawn adaptation and consider advocating for occupancies that organically grow and change over time. Likewise, it is important for designers to understand narratives of places and users as they seek effective ways to contextualize design problems[29] and embrace more nuanced, porous, and adaptive ways of intervening in the built environment. They will need to better anticipate diverse forms of appropriation that take root within the buildings and spaces that they design. By celebrating the inherent value of informal adaptions in an era of diminishing resources, designers can recalibrate their agency by supporting regenerative, emergent forms of urbanism.

ENDNOTES:

1 Christopher V. Hill, South Asia: An Environmental History (Santa Barbara: ABC-CLIO Publishing, 2008), pp. 35–38.

2 Vinayak Bharne and Krupali Krusche, Rediscovering the Hindu Temple: The Sacred Architecture and Urbanism of India (Newcastle-upon-Tyne: Cambridge Scholars Publishing), 2012, p. 19.

3 Alison Behnke, Angkor Wat (Minneapolis:Twenty-First Century Books, 2008), pp. 24–25.

4 Lauren C. Heberle and Susan M. Opp, Local Sustainable Urban Development in a Globalized World (London: Routledge, 2008), p. 177.

5 Vinayak Bharne, The Emerging Asian City (London: Routledge, 2013), pp. 86–89.

6 Esther Leslie, "Ruin and Rubble in the Arcades," *Walter Benjamin and the Arcades Project*,(2006), pp. 87–89.

7 Walter Benjamin and Michael W. Jennings, The Writer of Modern Life: Essays on Charles Baudelaire (Cambridge, MA: Belknap Press), 2006, pp. 2–8.

8 Hsiao-yen Peng, Dandyism and Transcultural Modernity: The Dandy, the Flaneur, and the Translator in 1930s Shanghai, Tokyo, and Paris (London: Routledge, 2015), p. 6–8.

9 Anna Budziak, Text, Body and Indeterminacy: The Doppelganger Selves in Pater and Wilde (Newcastle-upon-Tyne: Cambridge Scholars, 2008), pp. 47–52.

10 Michel Foucault, and Jay Miskowiec. "Of Other Spaces." *Diacritics* 16, no. 1 (1986): 22-27. doi:10.2307/464648.

11 Ibid.

12 Henri Lefebvre, Critique of Everyday Life, Volume II (Brooklyn: Verso, 2002), pp. 309–312.

13 Tom McDonough, Guy Debord and the Situationist International: Texts and Documents (Cambridge: The MIT Press, 2004), pp. 255–257.

14 Peter Burke, The New Cambridge Modern History: Volume 13 (Cambridge: Cambridge University Press, 1979), p. 357.

15 Agnieszka Sobocinska, "The Expedition's Afterlives: Echoes of Empire in Travel to Asia," *Expedition into Empire: Exploratory Journeys and the Making of the Modern World*, (2015), p. 227–228.

16 Ibid.

17 David Turnbull, "Soc. Culture: Singapore," *The Architecture of Fear*, (1997), p. 229.

18 Ibid.

19 Nicholas Grossman, Chronicle of Thailand: Headline News Since 1946 (Paris: Editions Didier Millet, 2009), p. 194.

20 Boonying Kongarchapatara and Randall Shannon, "Transformations in Thailand's Retailing Landscape: Public Policies, Regulations, and Strategies," *Retailing in Emerging Markets: A Policy and Strategy Perspective*, p. 7–9.

21 Mark Byrnes, "Removing Fish from a Surreal Abandoned Shopping Mall," *The Atlantic*, January 16, 2015.

22 Chris Pleasance, "Splashing out at the shops: Hundreds of fish take over abandoned Thai mall after it's flooded," *Daily Mail*, June 26, 2014.

23 Terry Fredrickson, "Bangkok's hidden fish pond," *Bangkok Post*, July 1, 2014.

24 Supoj Wancharoen, "A New World fish pond," *Bangkok Post*, June 30, 2014.

25 Sasha Goldstein, "Abandoned Bangkok shopping mall Becomes incredible koi pond after years of neglect," *New York Daily News*, July 1, 2014.

26 Ibid.

27 Supoj Wancharoen, "Fish pulled from New World pond," *Bangkok Post*, January 13, 2015.

28 Anthony Vidler, The Architectural Uncanny: Essays in the Modern Unhomely (Cambridge: The MIT Press, 1994), pp. 3–5.

29 Tasoulla Hadjiyanni, "Rethinking Culture in Interior Design Pedagogy: The Potential Beyond CIDA Standard 2g," *Journal of Interior Design,* Volume 38, Number 3 (2013), pp. viii–xi.

T-HOUSE

WATER AS MEDIUM IN INTERVENTIONS AND ADAPTIVE REUSE

by KATHERINE BAMBRICK & BRIAN AMBROZIAK

Located on the tip of Hains Point in Washington, D.C., the theoretical design project entitled *T-HOUSE* is an experience-based construct that juxtaposes two distinct landscapes and speaks to the memory of the 20th century teahouse that once existed there. The proposal encourages a critical dialogue between the natural and artificial processes inherent in the history of the site, from the engineering staged to control flooding to the articulated tea ceremonies that took place there. At each scale, the medium of water — its forces, textures, tastes, thermal properties, associative potential, and trace memory — plays a requisite role. Through critique of such qualities, *T-HOUSE* translates the archeological as well as environmental realities and fictions of place. It expands upon traditional architectural practice by finding root in some of the more primordial conditions of the human psyche, affecting the body through tactile means, responding to time and change in values, and offering an opportunity to transform reality.

Key physical and phenomenological conditions associated with water — *transformation*, *temporality* and the rhythmic structures of *time*, and multi-sensory *tactility* — come together as fundamental "T" forces in the *T-HOUSE* narrative. These themes are integral to the analyses of the landscape, program, and material investigations that provided motive for representation methods and context for the design. Design elements through which the story is told include a productive landscape supporting the intentional acts of harvesting, brewing, and drinking tea, a tight grid of irrigation sprinklers that emit domes of mist, and oxidizing metal skins, akin to the earthenware tea kettle that is ceremonially bathed in its own contents as an act preserving both material and cultural memory. With the environments of a productive landscape and an abstracted teahouse, this design accentuates the properties and aesthetics of the various forms of water as a framework for a new architectural construct.

I. Constructed Terrain

Context and artifact both play a part in the unfolding of the Hains Point story and are translated as evolving specters to become experiential counterpoints of the *T-HOUSE* intervention. The site is a fabricated island located at the confluence of the Potomac and Anacostia Rivers. It is composed of the silty spoils that accumulated during the dredging of the Potomac when the Tidal Basin was constructed in the late 19th century. This civil engineering project, designed to control flooding and fetid runoff of Washington's original marshland environment, was overseen by Major General Peter C. Hains from whom it takes its name.

Championed by the McMillan Commission in 1902, Hains Point became a public park a decade later at a time when tearooms were becoming popular in American culture. "There are few hours in life more agreeable than the hour dedicated to the ceremony known as afternoon tea."[2] The drink imbibed the nation in the years proceeding Prohibition. This also coincided with the rise of the automobile and recreational travel. In 1920, the Girl Scouts set up a refreshment stand in the park for motorists enjoying the "speedway," which set the wheels in motion for a more permanent teahouse structure built in 1923.[3]

It was mid-winter and the water's surface was covered with the withered leaves of the lotuses. Suddenly I realized that the flowers had not simply dried up, but that they embodied, in their decomposition, the fullness of life that would emerge again in their natural beauty.[1]

— HOUNSAI GENSHITSU SEN

While the location was ideal on the x-y coordinate map, in close proximity to the governmental and commercial hearts of Washington and Arlington, its vertical stance proved problematic. Unchecked by levies or keys, the extremes of the tides produced periodic flooding. After a generation, the teahouse fell victim to the fragility of the systems from which it originated. Materially, the aquatic abuse rendered it unsanitary; culturally, teahouses were becoming less fashionable.[4] In 1962, the Hains Point Teahouse closed and the structure was repurposed as a visitor center. After the flood of 1985 the building was permanently shut down and was demolished in 1987.

The story of water is integral to Hains Point and its social prominence through the mid-twentieth century. The landscape was created in response to the forces of a wetland ecology that existed prior to the urbanization of the area. To this day, flooding continues as a watery resurgence of nature's free will. However, rather than try to contest it, the Water Environment Federation and International Water Association have embraced the site as a water-rich resource by which people can reconnect to the watershed and monitor quality parameters.[5]

Hains Point is, and its teahouse structure was, a fabricated foreign entity. Yet, too, was the tea ceremony itself. As a ritual it is "a construction, a category or tool of analysis" that "has been pressed into service in an attempt to explain the roots of… human behavior in ways that are meaningful."[6] Tea is believed to have originated in China, date unknown;[7] the tea ceremony originated in Japan in the fifteenth century as a development of the Zen ritual.[8] It related consumption to meditation and aesthetics and suggested equality amongst differing economic and militant classes. In the United States, the tea ceremony held no such meaning. The tearoom was a fictitious stage where we found entertainment in the roles we played. Without the deep cultural roots, teahouses were bound to remain mere fashion and inevitably die as the trend lost favor.

These stories open doors to critical design investigations. Here, interest in adaptive reuse focuses less on the permanent physical elements of Hains Point and more on its temporal and changing situation. Water's ebb and flow suggest the potential to register new horizontal strata above the ground plane, defining alternate zones of occupation. Seasonal changes related to both human visitor and flora resident, one moving transitionally on and off the island, the other a permanent fixture delivering the textural palette for visual and olfactory encounters. We reconsidered tea not through its cultural association but rather its sensory potential responded to by carnal instincts. With these reconsiderations, we deduced that memory of place and artifact did not need to relate to just a history, but rather a contemporaneous evolving story.

II. Abode of the Unsymmetrical

> *"The Philosophy of Tea is not mere aestheticism in the ordinary acceptance of the term, for it expresses conjointly with ethics and religion our whole point of view about man and nature."*[9]
> — Kakuzo Okakura

Next to water, tea is the most widely consumed beverage in the world.[10] Originally sourced for its medical benefits, it has become a powerful economic and political commodity and has played a role in shaping the cultural identity of nations. Contemporary analysts of tea reference its prevalence in literature through the past two centuries. In the highly cited *Book of Tea*, Kakuzo Okakura describes tea as the root from which all culture is crafted. *Prix du Rayonnement* winner Francis-Noël Thomas introduces tea as more a recurrent side-note of life, present in simple gestures of friendship and courtship, revealing memories of the familiar with the taste of the madeleine.[11]

Tea consumption is practiced in as varied of ways as there are teas. As noted, the Japanese tea ceremony is the measure of cultural ritual, maintaining behaviors respondent to environment, season, time, hygiene, dress, even lighting levels and building materials. Exterior and interior threshold moments, *roji* (garden and path) and *tokonoma* (scroll alcove), supplement the *chashitsu* (tearoom enclosure) as places where occupants prepare themselves physically and mentally for the transformative practice of tea.

Besides serving as the solvent, water plays an especially important role in the tea ceremony as a purifying agent. Prior to consumption, guests wash their hands and insides of their mouths and often drink hot water, sometimes flavored with roasted barley. Utensils and vessels are prescriptively cleaned prior, during, and after use. These are then inspected by guests who handle them with brocaded clothes, allowing more tactile engagement to influence their visual perception.

Okakura describes the tearoom as the "Abode of the Unsymmetrical," purposely left unfinished for the patron's imagination to complete.[12] In part this term signifies the abstract disposition of the structure and interior design. It also speaks of the participant's need to interpret changes brought about by the spatial and material manipulation of the teahouse. Body posture and movement tempo are regulated through the ceremony. Chimes announce changes in phases. Open and closed doorways encourage air movement while stoked fires generate heat and produce enigmatic light contrasts. Often food and tobacco are served to offset the flavors of the tea and further stimulate the palette. Even interior scenes are modified during transitional stages as the host replaces representational scrolls with simple flower arrangement, signified replacing signifier.

These transitional moments are translated through sensory responses to the tea being consumed, affected by temperature changes, color saturation, aroma, and taste. Yet even without the ceremony, these tactile stimulants still produce a change in perception because they are intrinsic to the body rather than culturally learned.

III. Imperfect Waters

In the opening paragraph of *The Book of Tea*, Okakura states that Teaism, the practice of the tea ceremony representing the adoration of the beautiful recognized within the ordinary, is principally "a worship of the Imperfect."[13] In relation to water, this phrase may be interpreted in two seemingly contrary ways. When considering water in its most pure state, simply hydrogen and oxygen, there is an absence of any informative matter that could taint or provide evidence of context. Yet water is said to have memory, particulates of past experiences that may be described as imperfections. We find that water is not truly one or the other, but a happy juxtaposition of both.

The process of design is inherently a process of enjoyable investigation. During the time of the *T-House* study, much tea was drunk and much observation of leaves and powders and cloudy residues was performed. Most of the time we were adding substance to the liquid with expected results of increased color and opacity. But stepping back, it was the investigations of the "pure" water that most informed us of the nature of the imperfect. In its agitated liquid state, the solute particulates dissipate evenly throughout the liquid medium. Assuming a low level of saturation, this imperfect water appeared clear. However, by exploring the contrasting thermal processes of steaming/boiling or freezing, water's beauty as seen by its compositional imperfections was revealed.

Desalination is a purification process that removes particulates, particularly salts and other minerals, from *imperfect waters*. There are a number of techniques that may be used, from vapor-compression distillation to reverse osmosis. Following simple measures, we examined some of the most primitive methods that could be performed domestically. We set target thermal extremes as our first parameters, experimenting with reduction via steaming and material isolation via freezing.

Increasing the temperature of the fluid object speeds up the natural process of evaporation where the lighter, less affected molecules of pure water are released into the air as gas. In our studies, the steam rose as sensual overlapping atmospheric veils. If acquisition of the pure substance was our goal, we would have contained the vapor and condensed it. However, it was the residual fluid that inevitably held the greater aesthetic promise related to the imperfect. Trapped air was the first to leave the bath, violently emerging from the floor of the heated vessel. Rings of minerals formed along its vertical surfaces marking the absence of the departed liquid. Prior to boiling off the entire contents, we observed a subtle hint of murkiness as the heaviest solutes gained greater influence. For us, this was the point where the water took on its most imperfect and beautiful character.

Decreasing the temperature slows the water molecules more gradually and creates a more stable end product for observation. We started our second thermal experiment with cold water tainted with dried herbs and tea powders. By placing the vessels immediately in the freezer, we had hoped to capture the evolution of the tea infusion, expecting to see a color gradient emanating from the particulate source. The result was less than satisfying. Any promise of a subtle staining was obscured by the intense white that developed in the icy core. We began again, this time using ordinary water ice cubes and changing our method of observation from unaided visual examination to viewing via photogrammetry.

We used standard store-bought ice sourced from regional waters. The cubes were not completely transparent — their cores were marked by a translucent white. Mounding the ice in an area four-foot square, we took a series of photographs and ran them through a photogrammetry software that generated a digital surface model. With the physical eye, the photographs presented the expected geometries of angular solids and voids. Through the lens of the photogrammetry, however, we discovered new ice topographies. The software's digital eye was blind to the clear outer layers but could accurately decipher the minute detail of the ice's inner disturbances. The aggregate form of trapped veins of air and diluted solutes, pressured to the center as the outer shell of pure ice formed, offered great aesthetic and spatial consequences. So unlike the traditional wireframe that contains its described form, this newly created digital surface defined a territory that had no clear inside or outside. It was as if the dream of Piranesi's *Pianta di ampio magnifico collegio* had been realized through fluid dynamics.

This digital exploration helped us visualize potentials for a new topographic and atmospheric strata. We sought views within the wireframe that exploited characteristics specific to the molecular qualities of ice and exported these as flattened images in a series of plates. These abstracted images reinforced the concept of the *Unsymmetrical* as the visual similes activated our imaginations. We performed similar processes of digital abstraction on liquid tea and steam to capture each state of matter which further informed the design process.

IV. T-HOUSE

In *the Sphere and the Labyrinth*, Tafuri states, "The *collegio*... constitutes a giant question mark on the meaning of architectural composition: the 'clarity' of the planimetric choice is subtly eroded by the process with which the various parts engage in mutual dialogue; the single space secretly undermines the laws to which it pretends to subject itself."[14] In our experiment, the ice cubes created an artificial stability and required a new dialogue between the physical participants. This conversation acknowledged time and temperature, crack-lines and mineral veins, and most eloquently the reciprocal agreement forged between various blocks to accept either the inverse or converse form resulting from accelerated thermal processes. "Simmel... recognizes this in his *Metaphysics of Death*: 'The secret of form lies in the fact that it is a boundary; it is the thing itself and at the same time the cessation of the thing, the circumscribed territory in which the Being and the No-longer-being of the thing are one and the same.'"[15] It is our position that the physical state of water both blurs and accentuates internal divisions and its reading as simultaneously pure and imperfect adds even greater complexity to Simmel's study of boundary.

These premises of simultaneous boundaries and *the Unsymmetrical* inform the relationship between visitor and environment in the design investigation. While the idea of the *collegio* challenges traditional reading of poché in favor of a more atmospheric and changing zones of occupation, Teaism's assertions regarding *the Unsymmetrical* prompt a more interpretive phenomenological intent. We tested these assertions in the conceptual design of the *T-HOUSE* on Hains Point. The name of the work derives not only from the base ritual acts of tea preparation and consumption, integral to the site's history, but also from key physical and metaphysical conditions associated with water, these fundamental "T" forces being *transformation*, *temporality* and the rhythmic structures of *time*, and multi-sensory *tactility.*

Conceptually, the three physical states of water — gas, liquid, and solid — translate the archeological as well as environmental realities/fictions of the place.

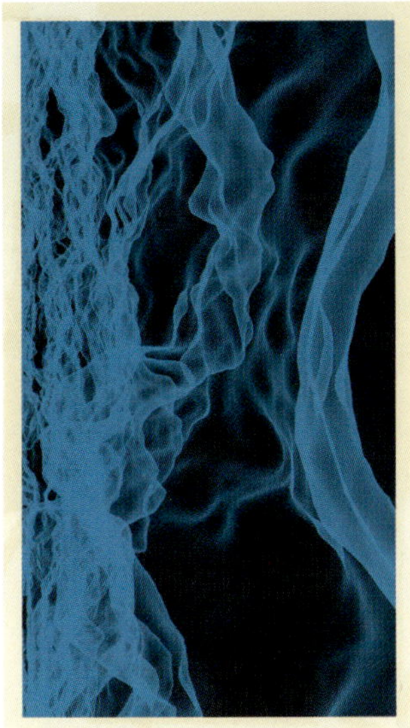
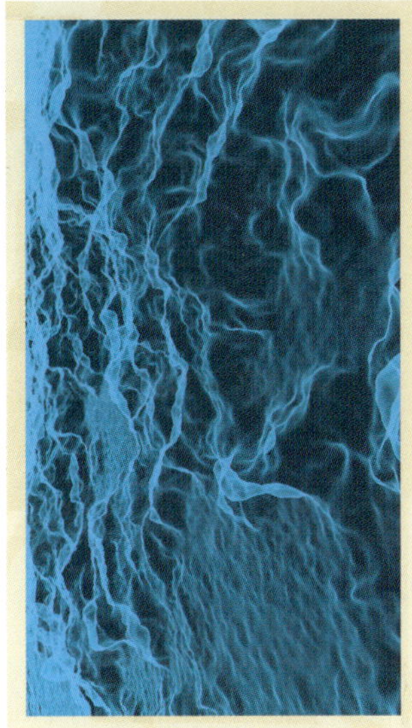

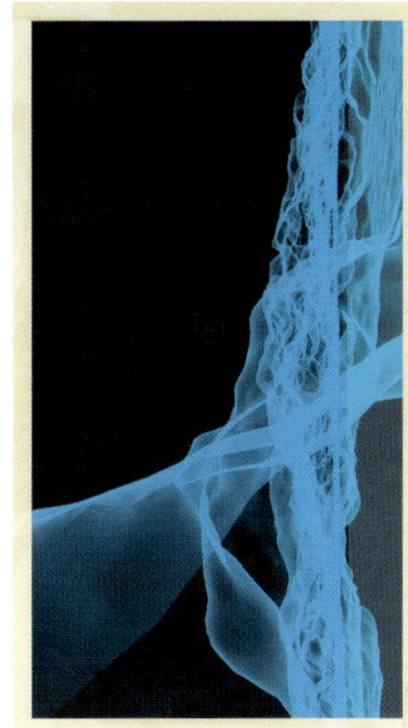

They relate in scale and association to the design elements of the proposal, a new productive landscape and a series of *T-HOUSE* environments that together represent a critical jump from abstract analytical exercises to resultant form.

The Productive Landscape describes a network of three ground-related systems: a planted landscape in service to the intentional act of harvesting, brewing, and drinking tea, a tight grid of irrigation sprinklers that emit domes of mist which define the zone of human occupancy, and woven movement routes that span across the gentle contours of the island.

The first lesson from Hains Point is the importance of water's ebb and flow that establish horizontal zones of perception. Here, atmospheres rise above the normative ground plane and suggest the true region of man's sensory occupation. One of the five categories for tea evaluation is aroma[16] determined by the volatile components[17] released into the air. In tea, these are transmitted to our olfactory organs via the steam that rises from the hot liquid. For the *T-HOUSE* landscape, we propose a translation of this medium in the form of mist irrigation. The spray of water droplets emitted by the sprinklers reach approximately ten feet in height, enough to suggest enclosure and an interiority of the exterior gardens. These water-defined rooms establish the Cartesian order through which the herb-planted gardens and meandering footpaths weave.

(temporality) The landscape follows the common diurnal, seasonal, and cosmic rhythms of time. The plant life flourishes and fades. Migrant birds and insects visit shortly. Holidays and weekends produce a greater deluge of tourists. Only the incessant on-off of the sprinklers is constant as a time-keeping element.

(tactility) It is a field of color, a mosaic of herbs and flowers enjoyed for their scents, flavors, and textures. We *touch* this landscape in the traditional sense with our skin and our gut. We *touch* this landscape with all our organic and motor systems as we transduce chemical signals into perception. We *feel* the memory of walking through a hot summer day, looking for shade, experiencing the purifying cloud of mist that regulates our body temperature and periodically fogs our vision. The water droplets refract the dense sunlight, producing an array of color that challenges the perennial blooms. We walk through this altered landscape and recognize it as both familiar and new, a memory and an experience.

The T-HOUSE is a spatial apparition occurring in series above the sunken grave of its 20th century predecessor. Resting just over the misting waves, the pavilions' folding metal envelopes allow a tenacious ambiguity between the visitors' occupation of landscape and room. It is here that the visitor enacts a self-guided tea ceremony with the herbs that only minutes before she has picked.

(temporality) The pavilions' skins are agents of time recording atmospheric, floral, and human interaction. Their low-gloss perforated copper registers the mist with fine lines of greens and blacks. Oils from the visitors' hands produce a protective layer and stop time where engagement is most prevalent. Traces of pollen and slow-growth algae produce a subtle yellowish hue on the lower portions of the panels, those most perceptible when one kneels for tea. We see this as patina, not corrosion. It is the focused association and ritualistic aesthetic of the conceptual teahouse.

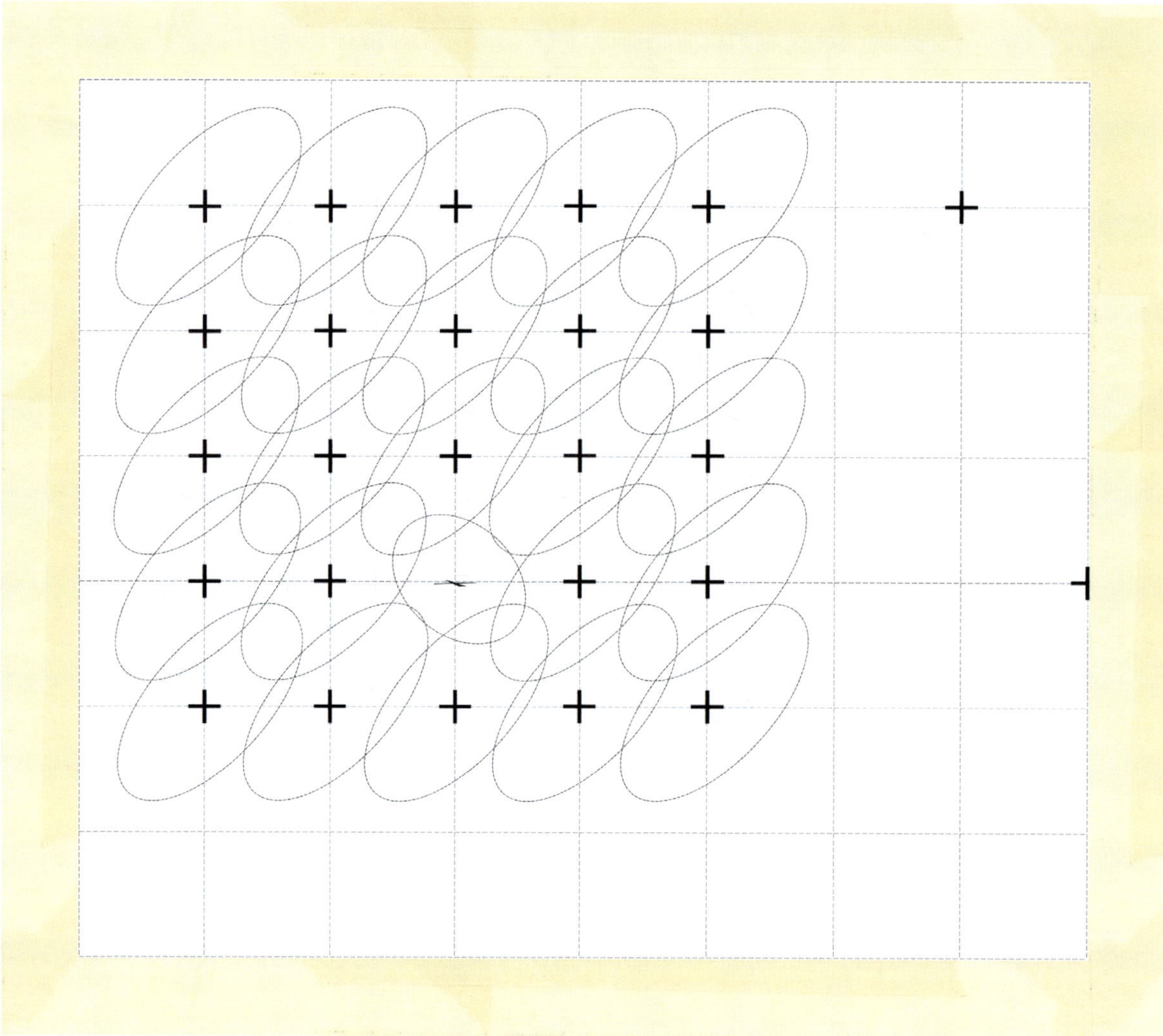

(tactility) Sensory agents are diminished within the confines of the *T-HOUSE*. The rooms are blanched, stripped of ornament and color to offer a neutralized context in which taste may be privileged. The floors are smooth and level. Light levels are balanced. Sound is muffled. Senses are stifled. A ceramic vessel, the self-selected herbs, and the steaming water are the sole contenders for the body's attention.

The Productive Landscape / The Tea House
Transition proposes two distinct environments that speak to the legacy of the island as a constructed landform responsible to a larger region of the Potomac delta and the ritual of the teahouse responsive to a society's values. Both these conditions have been tested over time and have known failure, yet the yearning to remember and adaptively reuse both land and situation are part of the cyclical story of the place.

(transformation) Set apart, these two realms form separate identities. They constitute liminal spaces with starkly contrasting sensory stimuli. Yet by their juxtaposition they are in dialogue. Our series of two, three, and four dimensional analytical techniques slowly uncovered a new *waterform* capable of superimposing the boundaries between solid and void, physical and psychological, and ultimately laid the foundation for a construct whose permanence evolves from its ever changing temporal nature. The visitor to this new realm is witness to the erosion of liminal states as interiority and exteriority are folded beyond one another to become the single entity. Such experience allows them to consciously enter into the continuum of this ever evolving story and themselves become transformed.

T_HOUSE productive landscape: irrigation grid

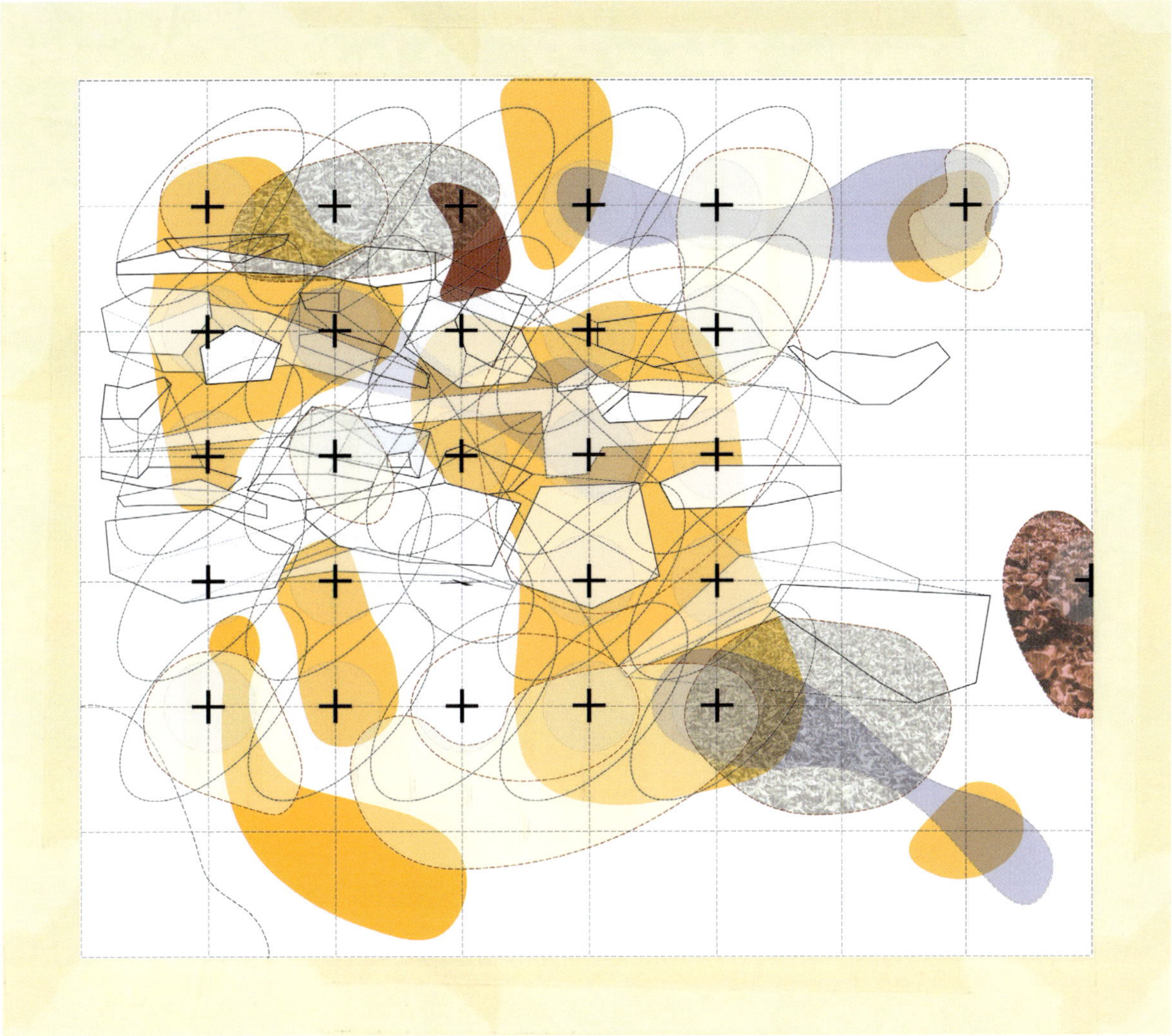

ENDNOTES:

1 Hounsai Genshitsu, afterward to *The Book of Tea*, by Kakuzo Okakura, trans. The Urasenke Foundation, Foreign Affairs Division Tokyo: Kodansha International, Ltd., 1989, 153.

2 Henry James, The Portrait of a Lady (New York: Random House, the Modern Library, 1851), 1.

3 John DeFerrari, "The Vanished Teahouse at Hains Point" (paper presented at the 40th Annual Conference on DC Historical Structures, Washington, D.C., Nov. 14-17, 2013).

4 Ibid.

5 "EPA, D.C. Area Students Officially Launch World Water Monitoring Day 2008." *US Newswire*, Alexandria, Virginia: 18 Sept. 2008.

6 Catherine Bell, Ritual: Perspectives and Dimensions (New York: Oxford University Press, 1997), 21.

7 J.R. Jackson, "Tea," *Nature*, July 14, 1870, 215.

8 Okakura, "III. Taoism and Zennism" in *The Book of Tea* Rutland, VT (Charles E. Tuttle Company, 1956), 35.

9 Okakura, "I. The Cup of Humanity" in *The Book of Tea,* 4.

10 B.L. Wedzicha, "Tea," *Nutrition & Food Science* 79, iss. 6 (1979): 2.

11 Francis-Noël, "Tea," *New England Review* 33, no. 1 (2012): 83.

12 Okakura, "IV. The Tea Room" in *The Book of Tea,* 54-55.

13 Okakura, "I. The Cup of Humanity" in *The Book of Tea*, 3.

14 Manfredo Tafuri, The Sphere and the Labyrinth: Avant-Gardes and Architecture from Piranesi to the 1970s (Cambridge: The MIT Press, 1992), 31.

15 Ibid., 5.

16 B.L. Wedzicha, "Tea," *Nutrition & Food Science* 79, iss. 6 (1979): 3.

17 Ibid., 4.

The 'Shepherd Path' of the Agro Tourism Albania project in Qeparo

THE BLUE LINE

REUSING TRADITIONAL RURAL WATER MANAGEMENT SYSTEMS

by FRANCESCO GAROFALO

Abstract
In the last century agriculture experienced a leap in scales, shifting from small scale production to large and mechanized industrial production. Such dramatic change has impacted local communities and associated traditional, agricultural techniques and infrastructures which have become, in many cases, derelict and abandoned. Traditional water infrastructures have been left behind, substituted by centralized large scale solutions. This paper investigates the importance of reusing traditional water management systems in order to create a resilient water supply chain, pinpointing the multifold benefits of preserving rural cultural heritage for agriculture and tourism. Traditional water management systems can become the link between rural communities, agriculture, and tourism — a concrete example of embracing heritage as a means for improvement and development.

Change of rural landscape: A leap in scales
In post-World War II Europe and, more generally, developed countries, agricultural production has changed dramatically in scale, specialization, and mechanization. From small scale farming, agriculture has moved towards large scale specialized production typical of 'agro-industry.' In developing countries the so called Green Revolution that occurred between the '30s and the '60s, resulted in 'new, high-yielding varieties (HYVs) of cereals, especially dwarf wheats and rices. These new varieties were developed in tandem with chemical fertilizers and agro-chemicals, and also with controlled water-supply (usually involving irrigation) and new methods of cultivation (including mechanization). All of these together were seen as a 'package of practices' to supersede 'traditional' technology and to be adopted as a whole.'[1] Such revolution resulted in an increase in water demand (for most of the high-yielding varieties), and the abandonment of small scale traditional water supply methods, shifting instead to large infrastructures for the support of the new scale-intensive farming. Large scale agricultural production has made derelict a great variety of irrigation channels, aqueducts, tanks, and wells that were the foundation of traditional agriculture. This has contributed to the further decay of areas abandoned due to the loss of jobs. The resultant movement to the city from industrialized agriculture has decreased the rural population from 66% in 1960 to 46% in 2015.[2]

Centralized vs. Decentralized
Of the global water supply, over 96% is saline; of the total freshwater supply, over 68% is locked up in ice and glaciers while another 30% of freshwater is in the ground. Thus, rivers and lakes that supply surface water for human use only constitute about 0.007% percent of total water, yet rivers are the primary source of human use.[3] Availability of freshwater is a current urgency for humankind, with the availability predicted to worsen in the near future. "By 2025, 31.8 billion people will experience absolute water scarcity and 2/3 of the world

could be living under a water stressed condition." Water availability is further threatened by overexploitation: "water use has been growing at more than twice the rate of population increase in the last century."[4] Climate change is increasing this stress, with the most serious impacts, which paradoxically can be expected at the same time, being an increase in the frequency and severity of flooding events[5] and a decrease in the availability of freshwater.[6]

Such huge demand of water for both domestic and agricultural uses has been supported by the development of centralized water management solutions which are now proving to have limits, especially in terms of expensive and inflexible long-term building and maintenance strategies. 'Centralized systems are not resilient in cases of damage because their structure is a chain of linked and interdependent parts'; while 'decentralized rainwater management, including retention, storage, and reuse strategies that are integrated into spatial planning and urban design, can reduce flood risks while simultaneously enhancing freshwater availability.'[7] Measures for decentralized water management are not meant to take the place of centralized systems, but they can complement them, improving the resilience of the water management system as a whole.

Reuse of traditional water supply system: New opportunities

Generations of villagers and farmers located in areas affected by water scarcity have been developing techniques and solutions for rainwater collection and reuse throughout history, making certain rural (as well as partially urban) civilizations independent and self-sufficient in terms of water supply. There is a great heritage of rural artefacts and infrastructures that were developed in water-scarce areas. They have now been overtaken in the past decades by centralized systems that render them redundant and, therefore, derelict.

These old, vernacular systems are of critical importance in many ways. First of all, they can complement (and integrate into) centralized systems, making the water supply chain more resilient. Secondly, such infrastructures are, in many cases, part of the cultural heritage of rural civilizations and, therefore, create a link to the identity of rural communities. Returning such infrastructure to use would preserve and maintain the relevance of such cultural heritage and knowledge. This is the case of Battir, a Palestinian village in the West Bank, located to the SouthWest of Jerusalem. Its landscape is characterized by stonewall terraces that are either dry — planted with grapevines and olive trees — or irrigated, enabling intensive market gardening. The irrigation is served by a 4,000-year-old elaborate channel system that collects and distributes water coming from natural stream sources. Battir was designated UNESCO World Heritage Site in 2014 for outstanding universal values: "The complex irrigation system of this water supply has led to the creation of dry walls terraces which may have been exploited since antiquity. The agricultural terraces, exploiting this irrigation system, were the basis for a strong presence of agriculture through the cultivation of olives and vegetables. The area still today has the same use."[8]

The striking cultural landscape is, in fact, still in use; the ancient water supplies have molded a landscape which is still cultivated with different crops, establishing a virtuous cycle that has made Battir an outstanding agricultural and cultural site, as well as touristic attraction: an example of balanced—sustainable—interaction between community, landscape and natural resources.

Another best-case can be found in the Indian *Kattas*, dams built by farmers across creeks to store water, once popular in the Kerala and Karnataka states. Made of stones and mud, these low-cost dams are temporary so that they can be dismantled before the monsoon arrives. With the arrival of running water, this practice has largely been abandoned. *Kattas* were part of the local rural culture and implied a savoir-faire, which has become lost in time. The cultural importance of such engineering works and the need for complementing the current water supply infrastructure are, now pushed by campaigners for cultural preservation, bringing the traditional system back to life. Workshops have been organized where farmers could meet and share their experiences, reinforcing the rural communities whose identities are threatened by industrialized agriculture. Besides being the platform to recall and share the *Kattas*' construction techniques, the workshop becomes an opportunity to improve the structures by the consideration of different material options. New *Kattas* have been appearing in the last years, with bottom up processes, led by local communities. Despite these developments *Kattas* have not been integrated into the government's water conservation awareness programs.

The conditions for reusing traditional water infrastructures require both a platform where the community can meet and interact, and seed capital (in the form of subsidies) in order to bring such systems back to life. What is crucial in each different situation is to act before the local knowledge and savoir-faire become lost. The advantages are clear and multi-fold: traditional rural water management systems are usually small in scale and low cost, which makes the construction feasible and quick.

Furthermore, traditional water artefacts can be linked with tourism alongside the territories for which they are best suited, including associated landscapes and local products.

An example is a rural development strategy developed for the Albanian village of Qeparo by a multidisciplinary team (formed by: Openfabric, MVO Nederland, Cityförster, Alterra, Sawadee, Boer Bos, GutundGut,

Arber Togani). Qeparo, located in the southern coast of the country, has always been linked to the nearby village of Borsh by economic and cultural ties. These ties became 'physical' when, in the '40s, an irrigation channel was built, bringing water from Borsh downhill to Qeparo, irrigating a lush terraced landscape defined by the cultivation of citrus and olive trees. If reactivated, as proposed, the old irrigation channel bears the potential of restoring the now abandoned terraces by creating continuous irrigation.

By providing an amount of water ranging from 9.660-20.125 cubic meters, the channel can irrigate a surface of 161.000 sqm of terraces. With the channel restored, the summer irrigation demand can be solved, fostering a more intensive cultivation (mixed-farming) of the terraces and consequentially, better maintenance. This would result in a drastic improvement of both the local landscape aesthetic and its productive qualities. In addition, a simple path can run along the infrastructure rendering it accessible and creating a new alternative pedestrian connection between Qeparo and Borsh. By restoring the water inlet, the channel can feed the terraces and also serve as a touristic attraction.

In this case, the link between rural heritage in terms of water infrastructure and agro-tourism exploitation is evident. A clear connection can be drawn between water supply as traditional artefacts (both architecture and agriculture) and larger touristic and regional development strategies.

The blue line: sustainable landscapes, sustainable communities

This paper is not advocating for a return to past technologies. The need for large scale water infrastructure is clear, especially when it comes to supplying cities, villages and agricultural areas. At the same time, the limit of centralised water management systems is also clear, as is the relevance of decentralized small-scale solutions. This holds particularly true when the small-scale solutions complement the large-scale water supply network and favor an integrated yet independent resilient system. Applying systems of adaptive re-use to traditional water management solutions, besides serving to augment large infrastructure through the creation of diversity and redundancy, opens up a new range of opportunities.

Artefacts, as well as agricultural techniques and crop species' selection, have been developed through generations in balance with the environment. Exploiting the cultural value of water infrastructures can enhance tourism in rural areas, activate bottom-up processes for sharing knowledge, and strengthen rural communities that are suffering the 'invasion' of the agro industry. Through reuse, indigenous communities can preserve their heritage, built over time. Preserving and enhancing the role of rural communities can re-establish the often-lost direct relation between sustainable landscapes and sustainable communities.

Capillary water distribution supported by traditional small-scale solutions can be the backbone to support agro-biodiversity on small, even family-scaled farms, improving the water supply and giving farmers a potentially broader range of crops. Enabling the farmers to act directly in the direction of reused rainwater facilities gives them the responsibility of their water use, re-establishing a balance between supply and demand (critical for sustainability), that has been, in many cases, lost with progress. Empowerment is the first step towards reinforcing the awareness of being a responsible actor within a system of supply/demand.

Adaptive-reuse can be the tool for water to be a medium of a holistic approach on regional development: the (blue) line serves as a link between the cultural yet, pragmatic, and past and present infrastructures.

ENDNOTES:

1 B. H. Farmer, "Perspectives on the 'Green Revolution' in South Asia". *Modern Asian Studies*. 20 (01) (1986): 175–199.

2 World DataBank, World Bank. "Rural population (% of total population)". http://data.worldbank.org/indicator/SP.RUR.TOTL.ZS (accessed November 6th, 2016).

3 I. Shiklomnov;. "World fresh water resources" *Water in Crisis: a guide to the World's Fresh Water Resources* (New York, Oxford University Press).

4 UN, "International decade for action 'Water for life' 2005-2015". http://www.un.org/waterforlifedecade/scarcity.shtml (accessed November 6th, 2016).

5 A. De Sherbinin; A. Schiller; A. Pulsipher. "The vulnerability of global cities to climate hazards". *Environ. Urban*. 19, 2007, 26–39.

6 R. I. McDonald; P. Green; D. Balk; B. M. Fekete; C. Revenga; M. Todd; M. Montgomery, "Urban growth, climate change, and freshwater availability". *Proceedings of the National Academy of Science*. 108, 6312–6317, 2011.

7 T. Scheutze; L. Chelleri, "Integrating Decentralized Rainwater Management in Urban Planning and Design: Flood Resilient and Sustainable Water Management Using the Example of Coastal Cities in The Netherlands and Taiwan". *Water*, 5, 2013, 593-616.

8 UNESCO World Heritage Convention, "Palestine: Land of Olives and Vines — Cultural Landscape of Southern Jerusalem, Battir". http://whc.unesco.org/en/list/1492 (accessed December 4th, 2016).

9 Accessed December 4th 2016. https://hijazih.wordpress.com/palestine-walks/battir-walk/

10 Openfabric. 'Agro Tourism Albania'. Openfabric. Accessed December 4th 2016. http://www.openfabric.eu/projects/agro-tourism-albania-qeparo-albania/

ENVIRONMENTAL IDENTITY

THE SÃO PAULO RIVERS CASE

by ANNE SCHRAIBER

The presence of water bodies in the city of São Paulo has been nearly eradicated over its history of periods of massive modernization and urban intervention. Even though some historical moments have seen the waterways assume a more important role in the organization of the urban space, as well as an identity factor, the city's development thwarted the citizens' environmental perception. The history of the city of São Paulo runs, however, in parallel with the history of its rivers, which, unfortunately, are invisible to us nowadays. The acknowledgement of the city's development, in tandem with its relationship to the water bodies, is a path to the recovery and preservation of its memory. Many proposals for urban solutions, as well as some interventions, have been put forward over the last few years. Having the narrative of history at hand is indispensable for the understanding of the proposals and interventions that attempt to recover this fundamental asset. It is important to point out that the resurgence of water bodies is seen as one of the major factors in the transformation of the city of São Paulo into a sustainable environment once again.

> *Knowledge of the history of a city, of its natural landscape as an environmental identity, indicates that, in spite of its many transformations and layers, each territory retains unchangeable features that may still be recovered. (CARVALHO, 2010)*

At the time of the Portuguese colonization in the early 17th century, the main rivers of São Paulo were navigable. The local bands of settlers known as *bandeirantes* used the rivers for their reconnaissance expeditions at the hinterlands, to search for natural riches and to conquer lands. During the Imperial period, the water bodies were also valued as an indispensable means of survival, so the city eventually grew in between the rivers Anhangabaú, Tietê and Tamanduateí: the former was a source of food and water while the latter two provided a means of transportation. At that time, the city encompassed an area comprised of 3,000 waterways, among rivers, streams and creeks.

In 1870, immigrants realized the river's potential as a medium for sports and leisure, having established the first yacht clubs, and enjoying swimming and fishing activities in a completely non-polluted environment. After 1880, however, São Paulo witnessed the industrialization and modernization of urban services, with political forces driven toward the creation of the necessary infrastructure for the economic expansion of the city. This resulted in the canalization of several rivers and streams, harshly interfering with the natural environment.

As a result of the transposition and canalization of its main waterways, the rivers Tietê and Pinheiros, as large avenues built in the valley riverbeds, the city is now facing serious environmental consequences. The rivers have become a problem for the city, which must now deal with the stench and the pollution everyday, as well as the inundations that their silted-up margins cause from time to time. The pollution and stench of the Tietê and Pinheiros rivers are the result of urban sewage being unloaded in their waters, whether by the rains that wash away garbage from the streets or by clandestine and legal sewage that still fail to undergo treatment before getting ejected into the rivers, affecting their ecosystems. In the summer, when rainfall levels are higher, the rivers overflow, causing large-scale floods.

Some isolated projects for de-polluting the river and containing inundations were implemented since the 1990s; however, they are long-term solutions and not entirely successful. Nor were they integrated efforts to recover the rivers and highlight their

caiaques, Eduardo Srur

importance as an environmental identity for the city. Traffic flow solutions overtook the rivers in the scale of priorities, rendering them invisible, and efforts to solve the physical problems resulting from bad planning, one by one, became the greater goal.

Some architects, however, have elaborated and proposed some integrated urban proposals. Oscar Niemeyer was a pioneer, in 1986, putting forward a project that recovered one of the margins of the Tietê River, in an attempt to promote reconciliation between the river and the city. He proposed the creation of a park with the construction of a cultural complex, leisure and sports clubs, residences and office buildings integrated with the landscape.

In 1998, the Institute of Architects of Brazil opened a public competition for solutions for the urban and landscape re-structuring of the highways at the margins of the rivers Pinheiros and Tietê. The competition sought ideas, with the goal of discussing the subject, but did not necessarily include the commissioning of the project. Architect Bruno Padovano, the winner, proposed the recovery of the vegetation and the improvement of the margins with the construction of a touristic leisure and entertainment complex as well as the creation of harbors for river-borne transportation, suggesting a public-private partnership for its execution. In total, 21 projects were presented.

In 2007, professor and architect Pérola Brocanello, in her doctoral thesis, established guidelines for the ecological recovery of the city. She proposed the creation of linear parks and the resurgence of the waters, which would make up a cooling system, increase the permeability of the soil and contain the existing major inundations.

All the projects include the tentative recovery of identity between city and rivers, whether through the creation of Niemeyer's clubs, Padovano's fluvial transportation or Pérola's extensive linear greenery. By proposing the resurgence of the waters in the city's environmental landscape, they all revive their historical importance in our collective minds.

It is important to highlight that all those large-scale urban projects have been elaborated without the involvement of the population; they were discussed among professionals, holders of prizes and/or notoriety in their field. However, it is a peculiar situation, that the existence of projects including expropriation and demolition at this scale would not be based in a more participatory planning process. The invitation of the population, hearing them before making strategic decisions in city planning, not only avoids future conflict but also creates a veritable

mobilizing force for such projects to be effectively implemented in the future. In order for this to become a reality, the citizens must have complete social and environmental awareness, while, at present, most of them are disconnected from the problems of the metropolis.

The work of Brazilian artist Eduardo Srur, that puts the driving force of art to work, was the only one of various proposals that was realized, however ephemeral, at the margins of the river. Srur found the motivation for his work in the contrast between the natural environment of the coast, his usual weekend retreat, and the pollution of the Pinheiros River, which can be seen from the window of his studio. Famous for his ephemeral urban installations, Srur creates conceptual and critical art by breaking away from the institutional boundaries of galleries and museums. His work appropriates the city as an experimental laboratory and calls the public's attention to environmental issues in the metropolis while improving the daily lives of the citizens through art.

His first installation using the river as platform in 2006 was driven by the behavior of millions of people crossing the bridges everyday between the branches of the highway along the banks of the Pinheiros River. This highway is one of the most important structural elements in the city's road system and is chronically the location of traffic jams at rush hour. The public seems to be completely anaesthetized, though, as they go on their way, too caught up on their own affairs to notice the presence of the river and its deplorable condition, except for the awful stench that emanates from it. This situation underscores the lack of memory, identity and ecological awareness of the citizens of São Paulo. Eduardo Srur, then, sought to cause a disturbance that causes one to notice and question one's surroundings, thus transforming one's perception of space. The situation of the city's bodies of water is, after all, a result of society's foibles and government neglect.

With his work entitled *caiaques* (kayaks), Srur makes an attempt to re-establish the connection between the citizens and the river by reviving the memory of the sport, which was practiced until the 1920s, when the pollution of the river began. The art piece consists of 150 colorful plastic sculptures representing kayaks, manned by mannequin dolls, floating on the dirty river. An interesting development was that the solid garbage deposit on the waters began to organically re-arrange the sculptures, which lost their original form. The artist seeks to awaken people's imagination about the nature of that water and the ways it can enhance our quality of life.

Perhaps, with the acknowledgement of the features of the water bodies on small spaces, and later on larger public areas, water could make a resurgence on the city's landscape so that the population, by recognizing its value and the need for it, would demand the "urban structuring of bodies of water". (BROCANELLO, 2007)

For a second installation called PETS, in 2008, Srur came up with twenty gigantic inflatable sculptures shaped as soda bottles, distributed along the concrete shores of the Tietê River. It was commissioned by the Itaú Cultural Institute, a foundation owned by a major Brazilian bank. Those PET bottles, lit in the evenings, were not just symbolic of the issue of environmental degradation of one of the main landmarks of urban pollution in São Paulo, but also represented recycling in two different ways. It proposed a recycling process that takes place through the citizen's gaze, by which they stop to look at the river that was once invisible, day or night. The other aspect is that the installation itself was recyclable. At the end of the exhibition cycle of the installation, the materials used for the inflatable bottles were upcycled into backpacks designed by artist Jum Nakao and given out to public school students.

The students visited the installation by sailing down the river and participating in an environmental education program led by an NGO. This intervention demonstrates a case of the public and private sectors of society joining forces to raise environmental awareness, which is fundamental for the requalification of the area.

Environmental education is an important instrument in the construction of an environmentally pleasant city, where everyone is aware of their responsibilities and able to collaborate toward a better city. (BROCANELLO, 2007)

The integration of man and the natural environment is the preservation of water resources as well as the acknowledgement of their inherent value as such. Sruh's ephemeral intervention alludes to the importance of the role of culture in promoting the re-signification of the urban space. Major urban plans can only be accomplished with the full support and awareness of its citizens. When the population realizes the importance of that environment, the collective spirit will prevail and urban change will be considered a substantial matter.

Water is essential for human life and a healthy environment. Recovering an environmental identification of the citizens of São Paulo with their rivers becomes, then, a pressing measure so that the next generations may enjoy the benefits of a more sustainable city resulting from a balanced ecosystem in which water is appreciated as an indispensable factor for their quality of life.

PETS project, Eduardo Srur

Zaragoza Bridge Pavilion, Zaha Hadid

A METROPOLITAN PARK OF WATER

by RENZO LECARDANE & PAOLA LA SCALA

For three decades now, numerous urban renewal projects have been focused on European cities built on rivers, demonstrating how an interpretation of the urban and peri-urban areas is related to issues of high-quality ecological development and environmental sustainability. This connection places the majority of large projects involving river cities among new environmental practices, usually linked to big events, which are seen as tools for transforming the region and the image of the host city. In this context, fluvial cities are becoming increasingly aware of the natural environment which shapes the identity of the place and which demands ordinary and extra-ordinary renewal projects[1].

This paper, in pursuing two themes, aims to grasp the multiple inflections of the ambitious project of the Spanish city of Saragossa, which, in 2008, hosted the *International Expo*[2], integrating it into a strategy geared towards transformation of the river basin area: the river basin as object of study and the urban project for the event. The case-study chosen is emblematic of these two phenomena, especially as regards the position of Saragossa at the crossroads of four Spanish cities (Madrid, Barcelona, Bilbao and Valencia), which has helped advance its development since the beginning of the 1980s. Furthermore, the subsequent decade, from 1990 to the early years of the 21st century, signalled a step forward for the city and the river valley of the Ebro, with the arrival of the High-Speed railway and the selection of Saragossa as candidate to host the 2008 International Exhibition.

The actual description of the event may well seem ephemeral by nature, but is permanent as regards the durability of the transformations, and sums up the contribution of the Saragossa Expo to the regeneration of the region. *Expo*, on the theme of *Water and Sustainable Development*, was designed to last and then to capitalize in the long term, and provided ample evidence of the skills that can be put to the test on occasions such as these. These events, in fact, not only permitted the city to show itself off as a whole, but also enabled it to confront its own physical dimension and that of the surrounding region, with environmental, social and cultural values added to the mix. Consequently, Saragossa suggested holding an Expo on the left bank of the River Ebro; the chief virtue of choosing this area lay in the opportunity to work on different levels of intervention, in the area's relationship with the river and other water courses and in the construction of a system of linear parks in the urban environment. Connected to the city, visually and physically, via new road-bridges and foot-bridges high above the water, the river-bank connected thematic squares and the *Water Park* to an ambitious global project combining green spaces with areas for recreational activity.

Not only did this project resurrect a recreational area, but it also became a bustling hive of activity in the large urban park. Agricultural working of the land was supplanted by operations on a grand scale, in order to resurrect, on the one hand, a vast area of marshy terrain and, on the other, to refurbish and enhance the eco-systems on the river-banks. The water-courses flowing through the city became natural and cultural elements of the new axes shaping the *Metropolitan Water Park* project, which represents the principal element in linking up the city's new processes of natural and urban redevelopment. The Saragossa Expo, by respecting the global phenomenon of great cultural events, incarnated the reciprocal relationship between the event (which aimed to transform the areas of water) and its resources, which this very region enhanced with a view to refurbishing its identity. The theme and its message, as chosen by the city, along with consideration

of environmental and urban resources, fuelled the theme of recycling of urban material, renaturation of embankments and the more complex theme of renovating the city.

The sustainable event as a developmental strategy

Referring to the contribution of the Great Exhibitions[3] in cities that have hosted them, allows one to insert Saragossa in the broadest national and international context, which, since 1888, has seen Spain among the nations most involved in organizing these cultural events of great import. The Universal, International and Regional Exhibitions organized in Spain were aimed almost exclusively at local people and heralded a search for an architectural style and local trends in the hosting cities. In this context, the Saragossa International Exhibition of 2008, as reported by the *Consortium Zaragoza Expo 2008*[3], developed a strategy in support of both the *Expo Integrated Plan* and actions to enhance the water-courses.

The planned operations, such as the construction of new railway stations capable of accommodating the new high-speed trains, all the new tertiary, technological and commercial areas and the modernization of basic infrastructure (including the international airport, navigable stretches on the River Ebro and the redevelopment of the *Canal Impérial*) were all duly completed; consequently, Saragossa contributed effectively to reinforcing its geographical centrality, both on the regional and national scales, and establishing modernization principles to improve the quality and quantity of public transport infrastructure and boosting the city's economy.

The challenge faced by the city, therefore, consisted in consolidating its regional role. This was based on its clear ambition to re-establish its centrality through innovative urban operations of national significance and with respect for the environment. These lines of thinking were supported by the strategic choice to address environmental development in harmony with urbanization along the river-banks and the river-valley of the Ebro. The backbone of the system of water-courses and the spontaneous vegetation along the Ebro, the various tributaries Gállego, Huerva and the *Canal Impérial* with the two large parks of Valdespartera and Arcosur, did, in fact, form a still visible natural system, which countered the occupation of land by the recent urban sprawl. Further to this resistance, interest emerged in redeveloping the riverside and linking it up with the International Exhibition project over the vast marshy area of *Meandro* di *Ranillas*, west of Saragossa.

The urban project

The Saragossa *Expo* entered the annals of great Exhibitions and became a key tool for future transformations of the city, capable of generating structural changes that had been almost impossible to implement using ordinary planning tools. As a result of its geographical location, not far from the city centre and the new intermodal railway station, Expo represented the new structural centre of a larger project of urban regeneration (Blasco 2008)[4].

In line with the importance attached to the event's impact and legacy, Saragossa proposed that Expo become the pivotal element in the mosaic of operations envisaged for the city's natural and urban environment over the following decades. In fact, Expo mobilized extraordinary national, regional and municipal resources. Aragona's government committed itself to building the cultural and linking infrastructure, such as the Congress Centre, the Goya Space and improvements in the metropolitan and road networks. The government of Aragona and the Aragonese community also participated jointly in the environmental projects, to redevelop the embankments, the countryside and the nature reserve of Alfranca. The city of Saragossa purchased the 25 hectares of the *Recinto* of *Expo*, building new structures for the event, new access-points with linking road-bridges and footbridges over the river.

Once the hypothesis of creating a theme park had been abandoned (Masad, Guerrero Yeste 2008), the environmental predisposition and the water theme shaped the city's objectives and the eventual choice of Saragossa as the site of the Expo, based on an ambitious environmental project along the banks of the Ebro. The *Water Park* project by the landscape architect Christine Dalnoky was included in the programming, which envisaged the laying down of guide-lines for Expo and post-Expo[5]; in fact, this was a fragment of a large-scale urban operation geared towards consolidating the city's relationship with the river through the creation of an eco-system of green spaces linked up and included in natural surroundings. The traditional

Google Earth map of Zaragoza, Spain 6/15/2013

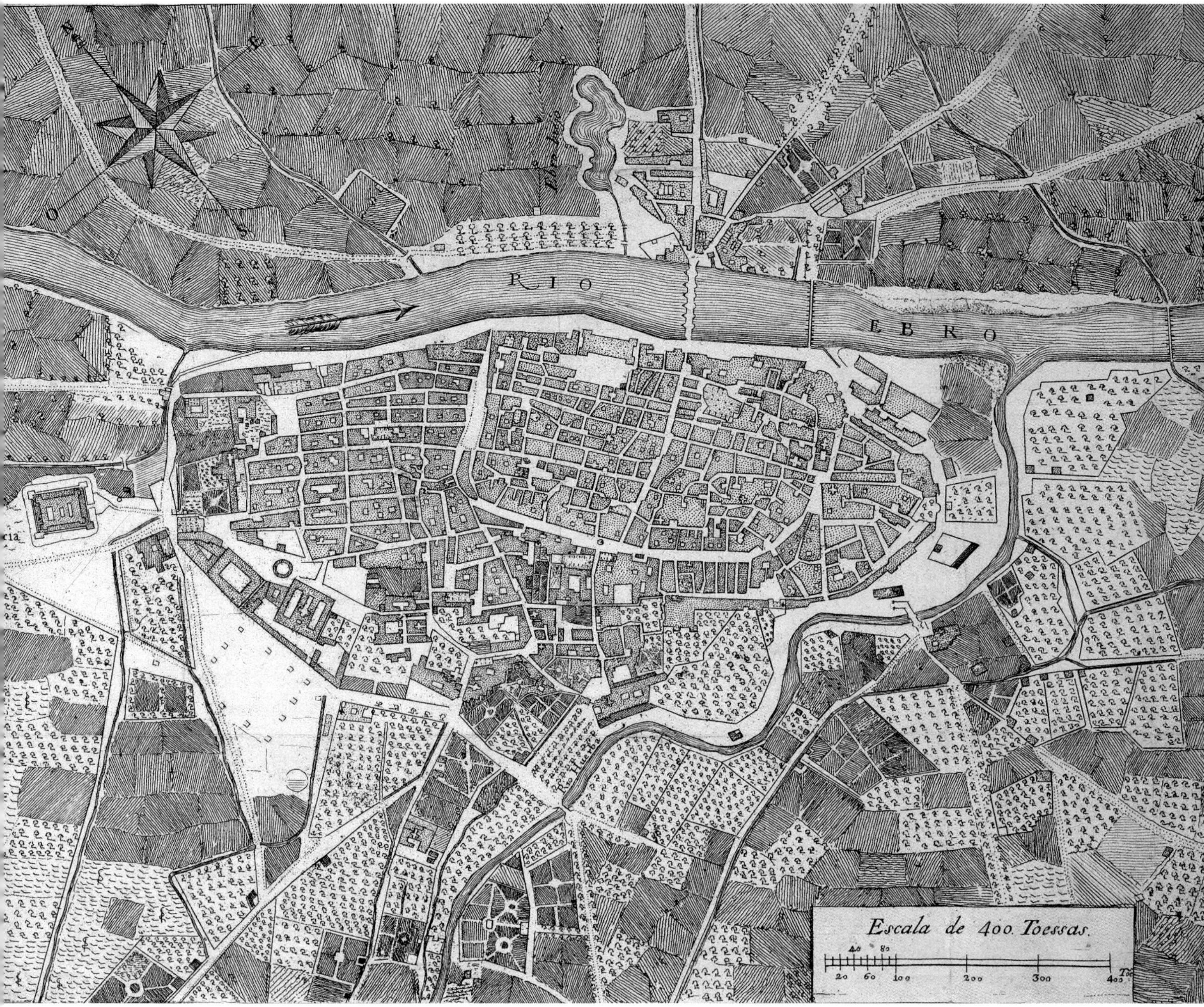

idea of the Park was here associated with open spaces destined to become a promenade connecting the green spaces with the areas for recreational activity. It was to be not only a place for relaxation and fun, but, above all, an *ecological park, a specific life-space and not an anecdotal park* (Dalnoky 2008), a concentration of leisure-time activities for urban society, in a place characterized by a large green space accommodating, within its borders, numerous areas for leisure-activities.

The vast Expo site today occupies about 145 hectares of the agricultural land of the *Meandro* di *Ranillas*; inside this, there is the *Recinto*, extending over 25 hectares, designed by the architects Enric Batle and Joan Roig. It opens out on to the Ebro and joins up with the right bank of the river via road-bridges, foot-bridges and the Pavilion-Bridge, the main access-point to the *Recinto,* designed by Zaha Hadid. Inside it, there are many buildings by architects of international renown: the International Pavilions by Azcárate y Banbó, the Spanish Pavilion by Francisco Magnado, the Aragon Pavilion by Olano y Mendo, the Congres Centre by Nieto y Sobejano, the Thematic Squares by Batlle y Royg, the

Plano topografico de la cuidad de Zaragoza del siglo XVIII

View of the Water Tower, Expo 2008

Expo Building by Basilio Tobías, the River Aquarium by Planchuelo y Coutant, the Water Tower by Enrique de Teresa, the Water-city Pavilion by Italo Rota, the Digital Pavilion by Carlo Ratti; the Funicular Railway by Hualde y Ramos and many more thematic constructions dotting the Water Park in the immense *Meandro* di *Ranillas*. All Pavilions are designed as flexible and multifunctional space where multi-sensorial, audiovisual and interactive exhibitions lead the spectators through an experience narrating the importance of water and its different uses in countries culture and history. We might also add the area of the Water Park to all these emblematic Expo buildings and it becomes evident that the contribution of the actual event, with all the political, economic and financial machinery set in motion, constituted the driving force for developing the city's riverside area, projecting in the direction of a vast environmental transformation plan.

Furthermore, in the wake of the construction of the AVE-*Delicias* railway station, numerous emblematic operations were carried out in urban and extra-urban settings, in service of certain specific themes. The issue of public space and its central role in the city was tackled in the redevelopment plan for the railway zone of *El Portillo*, approved in 2005, which envisaged the future construction of new residential buildings, services for both the city and the neighbourhood (offices, exhibition hall, auditorium and multi-media library), on the fringes of this area, as well as an outlying railway station. Then there was the theme of sustainability and innovation in support of the economy of the new Saragossa, which was tackled in planning the innovative and digital locality *Milla Digital*, in an open area on the River Ebro, between the areas of *Delicias* and *El Portillo*.

Fresh perspectives: towards 2020

The project described thus far was the challenge that Saragossa accepted via large-scale urban operations, in accordance with its environmental qualities, in an attempt to eradicate several blemishes on the urban picture; in this way, it inverted the previous radio-centric trend characterizing the city's outward expansion from the historical centre, in the years of the population explosion.

The events following the recent economic crisis, which hit Spain hard, put a stop to the dream of a short-term urban transformation and its anticipated, associated development. The present situation takes much of the blame for the difficulty in putting into operation the proposed post-Expo ideas, a plan which had been conceived before the event and implemented during it. However, it can be seen that the city has, nonetheless, shown that it has gained insight from the previous experiences of Spanish cities hosting similar events; consequently, it worked out a strategy of long-term interventions, geared towards activating virtuous processes of urban development. Moreover, in spite of the crisis, Expo did not represent an isolated event for the city. On the contrary, it constituted the beginning of a process of regeneration that rendered the relationship between the river and urban development mandatory, representing the first step in subsequent transformations.

Including the post-Expo period in its timeline, the 2006 Strategic Plan was proposed as the driving force behind the city's development up to 2010; it was to individuate a system of indicators to verify whether the pre-set aims had been achieved, so as to refine the planned strategy in accordance with the results obtained. Some positive data did emerge, being amassed during a series of checks immediately after Expo 2008, but contrary to general assumptions at the time, it appears that the economic crisis had a negative effect on both the socio-economic issues and those regarding urban transformation, which, hitherto, had not seemed to cause any anxiety. Precisely as a result of these observations, a new strategic document (*Estrategia 2020*) was prepared in 2011, with the duty of supervising the development of the city and the metropolitan area for a decade, and with a long-term thirty-year perspective, laying down some priority objectives: *integrating* nature in the city and in its area of influence, *improving* the air-quality, *bolstering* the development of clean technology, *adopting* operational systems for handling waste disposal, *improving* the water-quality and *reducing* its consumption.

ENDNOTES:

1 Cfr. R. Lecardane, "Fleuve en ville. Infrastructure touristiques à L'Expo 2008 Saragosse", *L'Infraville / Futurs des infrastructures*, (2011), 242-251

2 The International Exposition in Zaragoza proposal took shape and reached its official recognition during the municipal elections of 1999, through the electoral promises of Juan Alberto Belloch, Mayor candidate.

3 Entity responsible for coordination of all public administrations involved in the Expo. Cfr. *Bollettino Expoagua 2009*.

4 The definition of the different areas of the *Recinto* was built starting from the candidature project, presented in December 2004, which also included the successive reuse of the sites in a cultural and scientific park.

5 The Expo guideline assumed the integration of the river with the city in an irreversible manner following the principle of diffuse growth of cities along its fluvial margins. To this it added flexible planning, before and after the event, all the urban renewal operations, based on the principle of double temporality, launching a process of conversion of building in view of future works. The *Association for Strategic Development of Zaragoza* (*Ebrópolis*), responsible for elaborating the Expo guideline approved two strategic plans for Zaragoza, the first in 1998 and second in 2006.

BETWEEN RESILIENCY AND ADAPTATION

by CATHERINE JOSEPH

Each time there is a coastal storm event, architecture's position becomes that of a militaristic, tactical defense system. The storm is the opposing military; the high winds are the artillery fire; the storm surge is the cavalry; and the flooding is the infantry, swarming the ranks of architecture for one final defeat. Humans have been trained to see buildings as safe spaces: safe from climatic variations, both daily and seasonal; safe from most of the forces that nature repetitively exerts; safe from perceived dangers that roam our immediate referential universe. It is easy to envision architecture's position as victim of a militaristic climatic attack. What is more difficult to imagine are the ways that architecture can truly defend itself against such forces.[1]

Contemporary visions of architecture maintain the perspective, for the most part, that our buildings are designed and constructed to be eternal. As architects, we rarely visualize their demise, or the situation in which our design will meet its end. Demise for the sake of a philosophical architectural death is not the intent, nor is it a necessary outcome. Rather, the loss of a structure can be the result of a latent function that is designed to provide some benefit in its demise or its transformation.

In coastal scenarios — particularly those with threat of tropical storm damage — this might be a useful tactic to employ. Visualizing a building's end of life and anticipating potential modes of failure allows architects to design the building to either withstand the assault, or in a more incongruous case, to fail functionally in order to serve some protective purpose.

Just as one might interrogate material and elevation strategies in studies of flood mitigation and recovery, here too, the underlying cause for destruction must be identified and addressed. To understand the water-borne forces of tropical storms, one must first understand the basics of the destructive energy in water.

[destructive energy in water]

The National Oceanic and Atmospheric Administration defines a storm surge as an "abnormal rise of water generated by a storm, over and above the predicted astronomical tide." The atypical rise above standard tidal levels is an effect of both offshore meteorological conditions and localized winds.[2] To understand the potentially destructive capabilities of storm surges, it is useful to consider the conveyance and transference of energy within a storm system. Typically, waves are the result of wind passing over the surface of the water, transferring energy from air to water. Wave height is determined by the speed and duration of the wind, and the bathymetry of the water body. The water-borne forces that can cause architectural damage are a direct result of the energy input from the wind that is transferred first to surface waves, then to land. The energy that a wave contains is directly proportional to the square of the wave height. Thus, as wave height grows, as during a tropical storm, the energy contained in those waves grows exponentially. Significantly, although the storm surge undoubtedly brings a great deal of water mass with it, it is the transmission of energy, not mass, which is the focus here.[3]

[stronger is safer]

The destructive capacity of tropical storms is a given. Often, the most significant damage is caused by massive flooding. However, when Hurricanes Katrina and Sandy devastated New Orleans and New York, respectively, the initial disaster was caused by deadly storm surges. Similarly, when Typhoon Yolanda (Haiyan) struck Tacloban, Philippines in November 2013, the storm surge was the primary cause of the widespread destruction.[4] Since then, proposed strategies and policies have generally adopted a "stronger is safer" approach to coastal design. A 350-mile ring of protection around New Orleans — consisting of bigger, stronger levees, gigantic flood gates, and massive sea walls — was awarded $14 billion in federal aid.[5]

This effort to divorce architecture from its potentially destructive surroundings seems, at first, to be a logical solution. But what happens when these constructions fail, as during Hurricane Katrina? What happens where protective infrastructure is not a likely investment, as in Tacloban? Or when people have no option except to build exactly as before, with the poorest living over water because they cannot afford to own land? Architecture consistently falls victim to such events, amplifying the hardship and victimization of the people who see that architecture as safe space. Bulking up the coastline is an impulsive response that seeks to dominate nature and keep its dangers, and its many benefits, away from society.

[the sacrificial mindset]

The sacrificial mindset seems rather grotesque, but buildings are not living beings. Understanding their sacrifice means understanding the ways that we can alter our design process in order to accommodate an adaptive strategy. Although buildings themselves are not living beings, it is important to consider them to be part of a living ecological system. Achieving this means considering them as more than a one-time construction whose life-span is eternal and unchanging. Change is intrinsic to living systems; uncertainty, dynamism, and perceived imbalances are necessary characteristics of these systems.[6] If a system's response to a stimulant maintains a level of uncertainty, this implies an uncertainty in the effects that response will then provoke. In short, fluctuations within a system will occur, and it is this uncertainty that is typically neglected by architects.

Felix Guattari, in *The Three Ecologies*, discusses three complementary domains of ecology: social, mental, and environmental. Of great importance is Guattari's rejection of the notion that the psyche, the socius, and the environment are three separate entities that are acted on separately. Nature, he says, is inseparable from culture, and the relationship of anthroposystems, ecosystems, and referential universes must be considered transversely. This method of thinking across ecologies instead of within each allows contemporary designers to reconsider and reorient their strategies. It allows design to focus on the relationship of different entities instead of their individual, isolated functions.[7] This reorientation might also be categorized as systems thinking, as one is designing for anticipated events based on known relationship characteristics.

Ecological and systems thinking do not permit absolute control of the relationships among disparate systems and the events these relationships cause. Instead, they allow the considered analysis of interactions and permit speculative strategies that accommodate likely occurrences regarding potential reactions and affects. In adopting this mode of thought, we find that theories of resilience in ecology accept fluctuations and change as part of the process of equilibrium, not as an exception to it. Inherent in the acceptance and embodiment of this type of ecological thinking, and within any subsequent design strategy, is the acknowledgment of processes of constant change and adaptation within a system.

In acknowledging the dynamism of ecological systems, we see that the demise of certain components is inevitable. One might then question if that anticipated demise might be designed for, that the inevitable failure might be made functional. Designing for functional demise goes beyond the typical engineering design strategy of "design for failure." In designing *for* failure, engineers anticipate the multiple potential failure modes and the design accounts for each so that the design does *not* fail in that mode. There are a few engineers, however, who design their work to strategically fail. More specifically, failure here means that the design intelligently succumbs to applied forces instead of withstanding them.

[crumple zones]

Crumple zones of automobiles represent one type of design in which failure is embedded in the everyday function of the component or system. The components of the crumple zone of the car are staged such that the failure is a result of a certain event. More specifically, their demise is a function of the amount of force that is applied, and that they absorb. This embedded protection is a latent feature of automobiles. Most of us have likely owned automobiles in which this latent potential was never utilized (happily so). Although this latent potential exists silently for the life of the automobile, a more thorough thought exercise reveals that in order to design for the potential of a devastating collision, engineers must acknowledge fully that such an event could occur. The existence and considered design of the crumple zone itself acknowledges the grave danger that humans accept when they travel at high speeds in automobiles.

Consider an automobile moving at a constant rate toward a stationary object — another car, a tree, a telephone pole. In the time before the collision, there are no

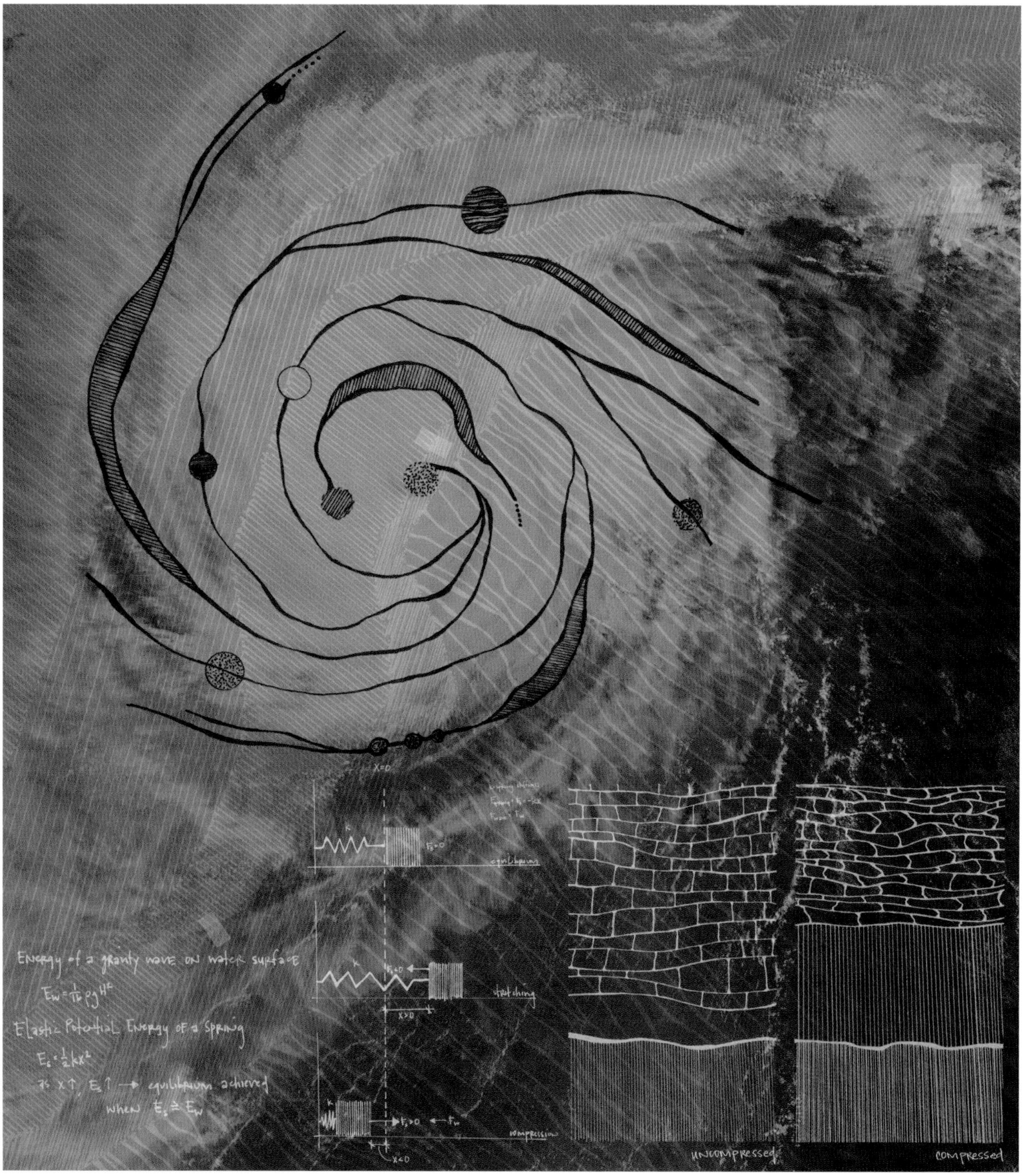

physical warning signs or indications that the body is moving towards demise (the human occupants, of course, can foresee the collision, but the automobile cannot). At some point, however, those moving bodies will collide and incur significant damage. This damage, in the form of kinetic energy, is ideally absorbed by the crumple zone. The folding of the crumple zone releases the energy of the collision as both heat and sound, decelerating the objects in the collision and protecting its human occupants. In this instance, the transfer of energy between the colliding bodies destroys the designed element, but activates its latent protective function.[8]

Architects might adopt a similar approach in rethinking designs for coastal protection, particularly in regions where the threat of water-borne destruction is a known, anticipated entity. In such an instance however, the crumple zone strategy might be applied to the stationary object (in this case, architecture) as protection from the moving body (here, storm surge). One might first consider designing for energy exchanges that can be predicted and calculated. Two such conditions have been identified and assigned the preliminary monikers of *Conversion* and *Absorption* for the sake of this text. In one, the force applied is absorbed through resistive measures that are somewhat more refined than a wall. In the other, kinetic energy is converted to potential energy and expended in a controlled manner during the storm event.

[conversion systems]

Conversion systems include those in which the transformation of energy is a means of dissipation and coastal protection. These might include water-turbines, or alterations to the bathymetry of the sea floor in order to affect the potential of a surge forming. Architecture may also provide some level of protection, if these alterations or energy-harvesting technologies are not viable. In its simplest form, the Conversion system might consider the conversion of kinetic energy to potential energy, which can then be expended in a controlled, intentional manner. The most basic example of this, one of the four simple machines, is the Inclined Plane. Very simply, as the wave front moves in, the wave's kinetic energy is expended as it moves up the inclined plane. The energy is converted to potential energy, which can be expended as the water moves back out to sea, or when the water drops over the upper edge of the inclined plane.

[absorption systems]

Absorption systems of protection operate via designs that integrate resistive constructions in which force can be absorbed. Consider a spring. Just as the energy contained in a wave is proportional to the square of the wave height, the energy contained in the spring, or the spring-loaded construction, is proportional to the square of the displacement distance. This energy, produced when the wave or storm surge causes displacement of the construction, is potential energy. Thus, the kinetic energy of the wave is converted to potential energy in the spring that can then be expended calmly. Given the rhythmic nature of the waves within a storm event, one can imagine a similar rhythm to the build-up and expenditure of potential energy within the Absorption system. As a wave front moves in, the kinetic energy is converted to potential energy within the system, and in the time between the wave fronts, the energy is expended in a controlled manner, allowing the system to recharge for the next incoming wave front.

The Conversion and Absorption systems of protection might take any number of forms. Only a few very literal, preliminary iterations have been shared here. The two Absorption systems are a spring-loaded hinge, and a compressible/expandable cellular structure. The Conversion system is the integration of inclined plane characteristics into architectural designs. These systems have been sketched in the accompanying images. To describe them further would require a presentation of the physics that characterizes them. This has been discussed previously. The integration of energy conversion and energy-absorption into coastal architectural design warrants further consideration as a method of ensuring safety.[9]

[design for functional demise]

Design for functional demise raises the question of social adaptation and social resilience. Social resilience is defined by Wu and Wu as the ability of a community to withstand, and to recover from external environmental, socioeconomic, and political shocks or perturbations.[10] Perhaps the most pertinent question regarding social adaptation with regards to architecture is: can social resilience be designed? Or must adaptive cities and architectural reinvention be deployed strategically within communities that already exhibit social resilience? If the composition of our built environment were to change, would it be necessary to teach humans to adapt, or would we innately adapt to the new spaces?

In this regard, again, Felix Guattari provides insight. His essay, "The Three Ecologies", highlights the importance of consistent and perpetual reinvention, seeming to encourage reinvention based on varying rhythms of repetition, the cadence of which will deter an entrapment in deathly repetition (which, of course, is different than the repetitive nature of reinvention). He discusses emergence and re-emergence, seeming to encourage reinvention based on varying rhythms of repetition, the cadence of which will also deter "deathly entrapment." He describes the effort

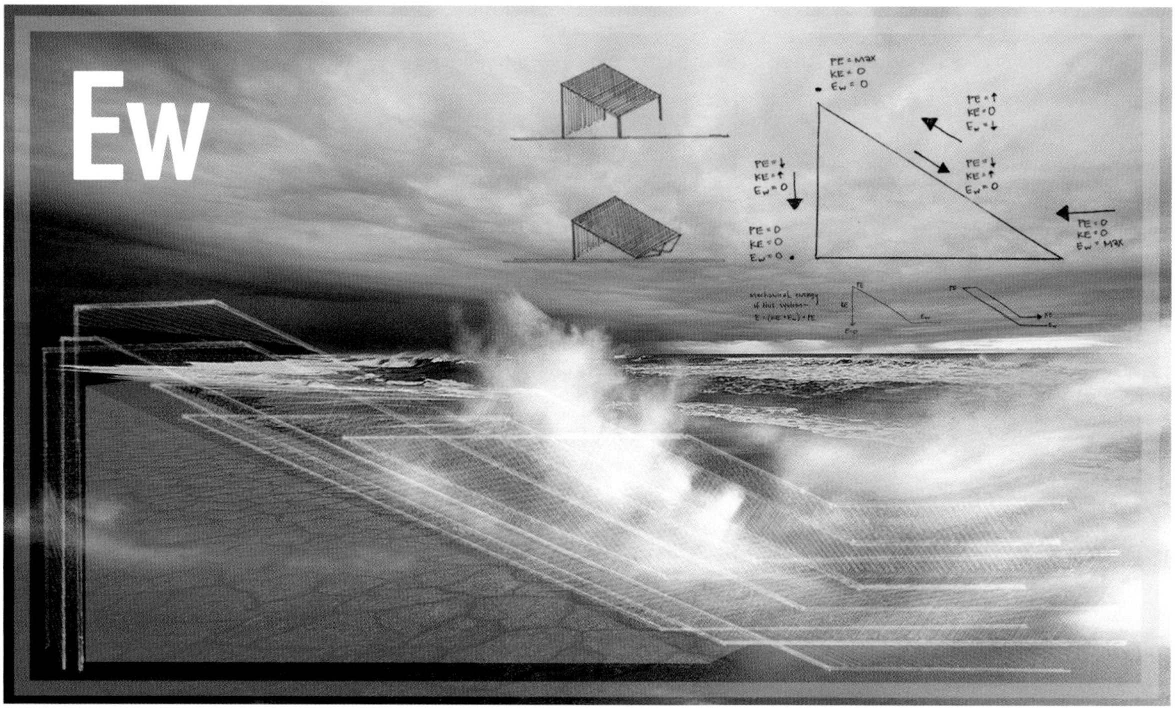

TOP
Inclined Plane
BOTTOM
Hinge

of repetition as 'mechanical,' bringing to mind visions of tedious but repetitive and effective mechanistic processes. He vocalizes support for continued inventiveness and the perpetuation of innovative practices. It is this alternative experimentation that can both respect the singular nature of the psyche and work towards the proliferation of an agency that can exist simultaneously as autonomous and collective.[7]

More significantly, however, Guattari presents a philosophy that relies on a level of social and cultural resilience that is unique to specific regions. This resilience is necessary for an amplified, perpetual reorganization and reinvention of our built environment. It is a repetition that is wholly different than Guattari's mechanical repetition, as it is a repeated reinvention of the built environment according to the conditions that exist at the time of rebuilding. The level of resilience and reinvention is a social expectation. One might consider that Guattari's mechanical repetition is currently how we engage in architecture, and is furthermore relevant when we design for coastal habitation. The question becomes, what sort of reinvention must architecture undertake to adapt to the changing regional characteristics and the needs of people who inhabit our buildings?[7]

Guattari's idea of repetitive rebuilding suggests the potential for a projective and progressive regeneration through the reconfiguration and development of what existed before. This way of thinking, reflecting the previously discussed ecological and systems thinking, amplifies the ideas that processes of disorganization and reorganization help society tend towards social order. This sort of thinking lies outside of what we currently think of as resilient architecture or coastal storm protection.

To say that architects must face the impending (and current) effects of a slowly shifting climate and thestorm events that accompany the phenomenon, is a statement that clearly underscores the potential of the field and the designers and practitioners that compose it. Architects, urban planners, and designers have an opportunity to rethink the way that our built environment functions, and the ways that we can further it to serve the people who inhabit and care for it. Anticipating and accepting potential damage and demise is necessary to design in anticipatory and conscientious ways. It requires understanding that damage or destruction cannot always be prevented, but that architects can design ways to transform the energy inputs and to mitigate the effect of the destructive forces. It hints at a design strategy that embeds latent adaptive and reactive performance into architecture. It speculates on an architectural design strategy that challenges notions of permanence, function, and safety.

ENDNOTES:

1 The topics presented here do not ignore policy and economic strategies, although this paper does. Instead, the ideas is to look beyond to tactical design methods that might provide additional protection during storm surge events, particularly in areas where retreat is not an economic or culturally viable option.

2 NOAA. "Storm Surge Overview", *National Hurricane Center | National Oceanic and Atmospheric Administration*. <http://www.nhc.noaa.gov/surge/>. (August 27, 2015).

3 Note that flooding as a destructive event is not addressed here. Rather, it is the forces associated with moving water (i.e. storm surges) that will be addressed.

4 "Mapping the Destruction of Typhoon Haiyan", *The New York Times*. November 11, 2013. <http://www.nytimes.com/interactive/2013/11/11/world/asia/typhoon-haiyan-map.html>

5 John Schwartz, "How to Save a Sinking Coast? Katrina Created a Laboratory", *The New York Times | Science*. August 7, 2015. <http://www.nytimes.com/2015/08/08/science/louisiana-10-years-after-hurricane-katrina.html?_r=0>.

6 Chris Reed, and N. Lister, "Parallel Genealogie.," *Projective ecologies*. (2014).

7 Félix Guattari, The Three Ecologies. 1989, Trans. Ian Pindar and Paul Sutton. (New Brunswick, NJ: Athlone P 2000).

8 Christopher Erickson, "Crumple Zones in Automobiles," Sourced through the American Institute of Physics. (accessed July 28, 2015).

9 Note that these proposals are for temporary structures, not for residential or other more permanent structures. Also note that the proposed temporary structures assume that all people have been evacuated to a secure, inland evacuation center at the time the storm event reaches the coast.

10 Jianguo Wu, and Tong Wu, "Ecological resilience as a foundation for urban design and sustainability." *Resilience in Ecology and Urban Design*, 2013, pp. 211-229.

WATER AS MEDIUM

ADAPTING WATER TOWERS

by INGE DONNÉ & BIE PLEVOETS

Water towers are monumental and eye catching structures in the urban and rural landscape, and until now serving the function of water distribution. Beside their landmark value, they are also witness of our industrial history as remarkable pieces of architecture and engineering. Technical developments in water distribution have, however, robbed the water tower of its function, resulting in the demolition of many of these architectural structures.

Our research explores the potential for adaptive reuse of water towers, as an alternative to demolition. We present an overview of the historical evolution of this impressive building type to gain insight to the fundamental characteristics of water towers. We also examine the main problems and issues related to the reuse and adaptation of water towers for new functions as a set of design parameters for this building typology.

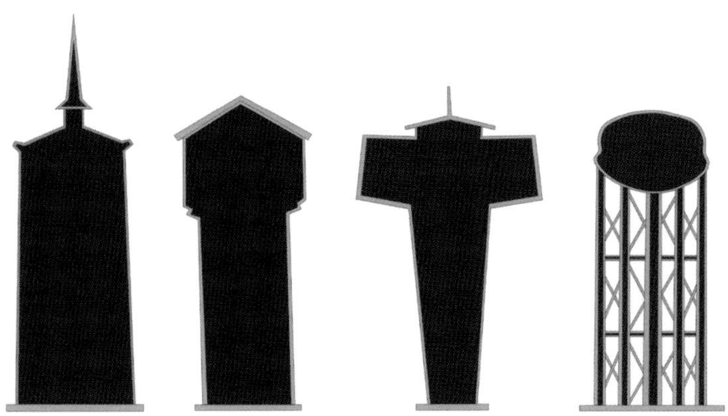

Historical evolution of water towers: materials, location and architectural style

The origin of the typology dates back to the first century, as an essential element in the Roman aqueduct system. As a high positioned water reservoir, it was used to store the water of a city after it had been transported through the aqueduct, so as to distribute it to the different districts. Since then, water towers have marked our landscapes and, in the course of history, the typology has evolved because of changing needs, technical development and varying aesthetic preferences.

During the nineteenth century, in the context of the industrial evolution, the water tower fulfilled an important role in industrial sites and infrastructure. For example, water towers were built near railways to provide water for steam trains. At that time, a water tower was nothing more than a primitive and cheap cast iron cube balancing on a structure made of bricks. They were of a functional construction and did not yet resemble the water towers we know nowadays.

Initially, the shape and outlook of water towers were not adapted to their context. At best, the cast iron water reservoir was covered with wooden slats. After the First World War, however, as water towers increasingly appeared in urban areas, a greater emphasis was placed on their aesthetical appearance: variations in colour and patterns of the brick work came to the fore, and later, also variations in shape and construction material. Trying to bring a unity with the existing architecture of cities, water towers started to blend perfectly in the urban landscape. Architectural styles and preferences influenced their appearance; for example, water towers

LEFT
Typological evolution of the water tower

RIGHT
Water tower in Delft (NL) reused as a meditation center by Richard Tombal architects

in the Art Nouveau style were no exception in Brussels by the turn of the twentieth century.

In the second half of the twentieth century, the development of the typology diverged. On the one hand, due to the increased popularity of suburban and rural residential areas, water towers were increasingly needed also in rural areas. As such they needed to be integrated in these landscapes. The importance of not devaluing the natural landscape developed a trend in the evolution of the typology, namely camouflaging; the water tower had to fade away in the landscape, resembling a rustic tower in natural stone, giving it the allure of an authentic monument. Every link to the actual function vanished by the introduction of this columnar shape, which differentiated rural from urban water towers. This type of water tower was, however, more expensive due to the large amount of material used for the base, compared to those water towers with an open structure. Therefore, this type soon became less popular. On the other hand, beside rural and urban landscapes, water towers were often used on industrial sites. These towers were constructed of steel and created with a minimal use of material. On isolated industrial sites, these water reservoirs, often spherical in shape, contrasted in character as a strange object.

Beside the influence of location, the evolution in building materials and construction techniques also strongly influenced the development of the typology. Following upon first primitive, cast iron water reservoirs, concrete water towers appeared between 1900-1920 as a concrete water reservoir hanging over a skeleton. The concrete material was still used in its very pure form, with a pompous skeleton, but in the following decades, due to the evolution of the material, the skeleton became slimmer and more elegant. As a form hanging over a skeleton, the function of 'water basin on high' was very prominent. In the 1960s, different variants with increased capacity emerged in the landscape: mushroom-, chantarel-, cone-, cylinder- and prisma-shapes.

Issues related to adaptive reuse of water towers

As many water towers have historical, architectural, or landscape values, adaptive reuse is a valuable alternative to demolition. Water towers, however, are difficult to adapt. Designed as functional infrastructure — a machine rather than a building with liveable interior spaces — the water tower and its floor area are limited to the water reservoir, although the base of the tower may be included in some cases. Further, the original circulation within the tower is designed for maintenance rather than for public access. Therefore, floor area limitations and vertical circulation are challenging elements for consideration in the redesign. Finally, the solid structure of the reservoir and the existence of the base do not allow for a relationship between interior and exterior. The challenges of 'opening' the solid structure are tempered by the loss of its main characteristic.

TOP
Water tower in Brasschaat (BE)

RIGHT
Water tower in Brasschaat (BE) transformed into a single family house by Crepain-Binst Architects

ROLE AS A LANDMARK

When the heritage value — including architectural, industrial, archaeological, scientific, historic, landscape, urban — of the water tower is very high, it may have a significant impact on the adaptive reuse potential and strategy. Indeed, sometimes it is not allowed nor desired to make openings in the structure to allow the incidence of daylight and create a view towards the surrounding, close the open structure, or add circulation at the outside of the building. In such cases, the selection of a new use should be one that complements the closed nature of a water tower and adapted without major infrastructural change. These include use as exhibition space, meditation place, indoor camping spot.

USEABLE AREA

For water towers where the base and reservoir are designed as one solid volume, the structure is usually divided into different floor levels, all of which can be used for the new function. Towers in which the reservoir is supported by an open frame, the useable area is limited to the reservoir, eventually subdivided in two or three floor levels. As an alternative the open supporting structure can be closed and used as interior space.

Adapted water tower in Brasschaat, Belgium

USE OF MATERIAL

In general, a water tower is a construction with a very pure and limited use of material. Initially constructed to be inaccessible to the public, the interior space of water towers is rough and basic, sometimes in contrast with its exterior appearence. The introduction of new materials with adaptive reuse needs to take into account the unity and sobriety of the original structure. Depending on the new use and desired atmosphere, new materials can be in contrast or harmony with the rough and functional materiality of the host space.

CIRCULATION

Water towers usually have a small spiral staircase in the centre, approximately 10 meters high and constructed for a minimal load. Additional circulation elements can be added as an internal stair or as an extra external element.

Water tower Sint-Jans convent, Overjissel (NL), transformed by Zecc Architects

INCIDENCE OF LIGHT

The transformation of the interior of the water tower to liveable spaces requires the introduction of daylight. Different design solutions exist for different types of towers. For towers with an open base, openings can be created through the enclosure of the base with opaque or transparent materials. In solid towers, openings may be created. However, the shape and position of these openings have a great impact on the out-look of the tower and its architectural and historical significance.

VIEW TOWARDS THE SURROUNDING

Beside the incidence of light, creating new openings in the structure of the water tower has another advantage: namely to give a view of the surrounding context. However, such views can also be accessed from the top of the tower or as observation platforms integrated into the new volume.

Water tower Sint-Jans convent, Overjissel (NL), transformed by Zecc Architects

PROJECT CREDITS, INFORMATION AND BIBLIOGRAPHIES

EDITORIAL

Project Name_Projecting Change

Image Credits: Neethi Abraham, Angelica Carvahales, Udeeta Jain, Mengran Jiang, Vinoti Kabara, Krishna Lingutla, Sneha Mathreja, Hana Mehta, Gloria Ramirez, Eshank Rishi, Eder Romero, Yinghua Tan, Rohit Vantaram, Ananya Vij, Plub Warnitchai, Mengyue Zhou

BREATHE, LOOK, STAND UP

Project Name 01_ DC ExchangeProject_Site_ McMillan Slow Sand Filtration site_ Location_ Washington DC_ New use 01_ Community center, marketplace, performance_ Project Name 02_ People's Liberation Army No. 1102_ Location_ Shenyang China_ Original architect_ Communist Party China_ Rehabilitation architect_ META-Project_ New use 02_ Exhibition space, mini theatre

Image Credits_ Figure 01,02, 08_ McMillan slow sand filtration site, Washington, DC, Lewis Francis; Figure 03 –07_ Public Folly, Shenyang, China, META-Project; Figure 09_ Courtesy of Lindsay Winstead

BIBLIOGRAPHY:

- Burian, S., J. Stephan Nix, Robert E. Pitt, S. Rocky Durrans. "Urban Wastewater Management in the United States: Past, Present, and Future". *Journal of Urban Technology* 7, no. 3 (2010): 33 – 62, https://dx.doi.org/10.1080%2F713684134.
- Cartwright, M. "Aqueduct — Definition." *Ancient History Encyclopedia*. 2012. http://www.ancient.eu /aqueduct/ (accessed September 5, 2016).
- EHT Traceries, Inc. *"McMillan Slow Sand Filtration Plant."* Historic Preservation Report for the Proposed Redevelopment of the McMillan Slow Sand Filtration Plant. 2010.
- Greenberg, S. *Invisible New York: The Hidden Infrastructure of the City.* London: The Johns Hopkins Press Ltd. 1998.
- Harper, D. "Infrastructure." *Online Etymology Dictionary*. http://dictionary.reference.com/browse/infrastructure (accessed January 10, 2014).
- Hobsbawm, E. *The Age of Revolution: Europe 1789-1848.* United Kingdom: Weidenfeld & Nicolson Ltd. Vintage Books, 1962.
- Jacobsen, T., and L. Seton. *Sennacherib's Aqueduct at Jerwan.* University of Chicago Press: Oriental Institute Publication. 1935.
- META-Project. "Public Folly — Water Tower Renovation PR Text." Dongcheng District, Beijing: August 5, 2013. September 3, 2016.
- META-Project. "Water Tower Renovation — Industrial Heritage Reuse." December 2012. http://www.meta-project.org/projectdetail?projectQueryCon.id=47&select=2,1 (accessed September 3, 2016).
- Metcalf, L.; Harrison P. Eddy. *"American Sewerage Practice."* New York: McGraw-Hill. Vol. I, Design of Sewers, 1914.
- "Public Folly — Water Tower Renovation / META – Project." *ArchDaily*. August 20, 2013. http://www.archdaily.com/417034/public-folly-water-tower-renovation-meta-project/ (accessed September 3, 2016).
- "Reference Terms — Infrastructure." *ScienceDaily*, 2006. https://www.sciencedaily.com/terms/infrastructure.htm.
- Rodda, J. C. and Lucio Ubertini. "The Basis of Civilization — Water Science?" International Association of Hydrological Sciences, 2004.
- Staley, Cady; George S. Pierson. *The Separate System of Sewerage, Its Theory and Construction*. New York: D. Van Nostrand Co. 1891.

THE TEARS OF THE U.S.S. ARIZONA

Project Name_ A tomb that lives; Location_ Pearl Harbor, Hawaii

Image Credits_ Figure 01_ View of USS ARIZONA taken from Manhattan Bridge on the East River in New York City on its way back from sea trials. December 25, 1916, Library of Congress Prints and Photographs Division Washington, D.C. 20540 USA http://hdl.loc.gov/loc.pnp/pp.print; photographer_Enrique Muller, Jr. / E. Muller; 1916; Wikimedia; Figure 02_ A TOMB THAT LIVES Monument proposal, illustration by author; Figure 03_An aerial view of the USS Arizona Memorial, U.S. Navy photo by Photographer's Mate 3rd Class Jayme Pastoric, Wikimedia

BIBLIOGRAPHY:

- Henderson, S. "Submerged Cultural Resources Study, USS Arizona Memorial and Pearl Harbor National Historic Landmark". Santa Fe, NM: Submerged Cultural Resources Unit.
- Shapiro, T. "Arizona Memorial Seen as a Dedication to Peace". *Honolulu Star Bulletin*. May. 2002. Southwest Cultural Resources Center. 1989. "Section IV: Biofouling and Corrosion Study."
- Stille, M., and A. Hook. *Yamamoto Isoroku: Leadership, Strategy, Conflict*. Oxford: Osprey. 2012.
- Stillwell, P. *Battleship Arizona: An Illustrated History.* Annapolis, MD. Naval Institute. 1991.
- The National World War Two Museum, New Orleans. "The D-Day Invasions in the Pacific". December 2001. http://www.nationalww2museum.org
- U.S.S. Arizona Preservation Project 2004, "Baseline Environmental Data Collection." http://128.146.17.149/previous-programs/Arizona/Legacy_2.html (accessed 10 December, 2016).

THE EDGE OF CONDITION

Project Name 01_ Three Mills_ Bromley-by-Bow_ River Lee_ London, England_ Project Name 02_ The White Building_ Lee Navigation Canal_ Hackney Wick_ Stratford, England,_Project Name 03_ The Marine Engine House_ Wlathamstow Reservoirs

Image Credits_ All images courtesy of the authors; Figure 01, 02_Three Mills Island, London_ Figure 03_ White Building_ Hackney Centre Wick_ Stratford_ Figure 04_ The Sinking Future Post Apocalyptic Flood Survival Centre.

BIBLIOGRAPHY:

- Bluestone, Daniel. "Challenges for Heritage Conservation and the role of Research on Values" In *Values and Heritage Conservation*, ed. Erica Avrami, Randall Mason, Marta de la Torre. Los Angeles: The Getty Conservation Institute, 2000.
- Evans, Graeme. "The Lee Valley: an industrial river system and heritage landscape". In Patrimonie Paesaggi : Costruiti Dall'acqua, ed. Margherita Vanore, 90 –101. Milano: Mim Edizioni Srl-Udine, 2016.
- Foucault, Michael. "Of Other Spaces: Utopias and Heterotopias," *Architecture, Mouvement, Continuité*. 5, 1984, 46 – 49.
- Hollis, Ed. *The Secret Lives of Buildings: From the Parthenon to the Vegas Strip in Thirteen Stories*. London: Portobello Books, 2010.
- Knight, Jasper. "Development of Palimpsest Landscapes", 2012, http://serc.carleton.edu/68942, (accessed December 16, 2016.)
- Lewis, Jim. *London's Lee Valley: Britain's Best Kept Secret*. Chichester: Phillimore & Co, 1999.
- Machado, Rodolfo. "Toward a Theory of Remodelling — Old Buildings as Palimpsest." *Progressive Architecture*. 11, no. 76, (1976): 48.
- Marshall, R. *Waterfronts in Post-Industrial Cities*. London: Spon, 2001.
- Norberg-Schulz, Christian. *Genius Loci: Towards a Phenomenology of*

Architecture. New York: Rizzoli, 1985.
- Norberg-Schulz, Christian. "The phenomenon of place." In *Theorizing a new agenda for architecture: an anthology of architectural theory 1965 – 1995*. ed. Kate Nesbitt. New York: Princeton Architectural Press, 1996.
- Pallasmaa, Juhani. *The Eyes of the Skin*. Chichester: J.Wiley & Sons, 1996.
- Solà-Morales, I de. "Terrain Vague." In *Anyplace*. ed. Cynthia C. Davidson. 118 – 123. Cambridge: MIT Press, 1995.
- Strong, Brian. "A tidal mill tale." *Journal of the Islington Archaeology & History Society* 4, no. 1 (2014): 16 – 17.
- Symmons Roberts, Michael & Paul Farley. *Edgelands*. London: Vintage, 2012.
- TICCIH (The International Committee for the Conservation of the Industrial Heritage), *Industrial Heritage Re-tooled: The TICCIH guide to Industrial Heritage Conservation*. James Douet (ed.) Lancaster: Carnegie. 2012. 236.
- Weizman, Eyal. *Forensic Architecture: Notes from Fields and Forums*. Kassel: *Documenta*. Series 062.

BACK TO THE FUTURE

Image Credits_ Figure 01_ The Big U, Courtesy of Bjarke Ingels Group; Figure 02, 03, 05) by Julia Casol; Figure 04_ Courtesy of H+N+S Landscape Architects; Figure 06_ Dijkdoorbraak bij Bemmel, 1799, Christiaan Josi, naar Jacob Cats (1741 – 1799), 1802, source: Rijksmuseum, Amsterdam

BIBLIOGRAPHY:

- de Vries, J. "The Netherlands and the polder model: Questioning the polder model concept." *BMGN — the Low Countries Historical Review* 129, no. 1 (2014): 99 – 111.
- Dutch Water Authorities. 2015. *Water Governance: The Dutch Water Authority Model*. URL: http://www.dutchwaterauthorities.com/wp-content/uploads/2015/05/Water-Governance-The-Dutch-Water-Authority-Model1.pdf (accessed August 30, 2016).
- Gunn, C. "Acequias as Commons: Lessons for a Post-Capitalist World." *Review of Radical Political Economics* 48, no. 1 (2016): 81 – 9.
- Lewis, M. E., and Craig L. Torbenson. "Cultural Antecedents of J. W. Powell's Arid Lands Report." *Journal of Geography* 89, no. 2 (1990): 74 – 80.
- Lokman, Kees. "Dam[ned] landscapes: Envisioning fluid geographies." *Journal of Architectural Education* 70, no. 1 (2016a): 6 – 12.
- Lokman, K. "Exploring a New Paradigm: Water management in Mexico City." *Topos: European Landscape Magazine*, no. 96 (2016b): 44 – 50.
- Lokman, K. "Progressive Pragmatism: The Next Generation of Dutch Landscape Design Practices." *Proceedings of the Cracow Landscape Conference*, (2016c): 19 – 28. http://www.clc.edu.pl/wp-content/uploads/2016/09/VOL_1_CLC2016.pdf
- Merlín-Uribe, Yair, et al. "Environmental and Socio-Economic Sustainability of Chinampas (Raised Beds) in Xochimilco, Mexico City." *International Journal of Agricultural Sustainability* 11, no. 3, (2013): 216.
- Parsons, J. R. "Political implications of prehispanic chinampas agriculture in the Valley of Mexico." In H.R. Harvey (ed.) *Land and politics in the Valley of Mexico. A two thousand year perspective*. Albuquerque: University of New Mexico Press, 1991.
- Powell, J. W. *Report on the lands of the arid region of the United States: With a more detailed account of the lands of Utah with maps*. Washington, DC: Government Printing Office, 1878.
- Raheem, N. "A Common-Pool Resource Experiment in Acequia Communities." *International Journal Of The Commons* 9, no. 1 (2015): 306 – 321.
- Raheem, Nejem. "A common-pool resource experiment in acequia communities." *International Journal of the Commons* 9 (1) (2015): 306 – 21.
- Salewski, C. *Dutch new worlds: Scenarios in physical planning and design in the Netherlands, 1970 – 2000*. Rotterdam: 010 Publishers, 2012.
- Sanders, William T., Robert S. Santley, and Jeffrey R. Parsons. *The Basin of Mexico: The Ecological Processes in the Evolution of a Civilization*. New York: Academic Press, 1979.
- Santistevan, M. "Acequia Culture and the Regional Food System." Coyote Gulch. URL: https://coyotegulch.blog/2016/10/16/acequia-culture-and-the-regional-food-system-miguel-santistevan/ (accessed November 15, 2016).
- Schmidt, JJ., and D. Shrubsole. "Modern Water Ethics: Implications for Shared Governance." *Environmental Values*, vol. 22, no. 3 (2013): 359 – 379.
- Torres-Lima, P., B. Canabal-Cristiani, and G. Burela-Rueda. "Urban Sustainable Agriculture: The Paradox of the Chinampa System in Mexico City." *Agriculture and Human Values* 11, no. 1 (1994): 37 – 46.
- van Tielhof, M. "Forced Solidarity: Maintenance of Coastal Defences Along the North Sea Coast in the Early Modern Period." *Environment and History* 21, no. 3 (2015): 319 – 350.
- Worster, D. "A River Running West: Reflections on John Wesley Powell." *Journal of Cultural Geography* 26, no. 2 (2009): 113 – 126.
- Zevenbergen, Chris, et al. "Taming Global Flood Disasters. Lessons Learned from Dutch Experience." *Natural Hazards* 65, no. 3 (2013): 1217 – 1225.

THE OYSTER BLOCKS PROJECT

Project Name_ The Oyster Blocks Project

Image Credits_ Figure 01 – 07_ courtesy of the author

BIBLIOGRAPHY:

- Agrest, D. "Design Versus Non-Design," *Oppositions*, no. 6 (1976).
- Christian, R., F. Steimle, and R. Stone. "Evolution of Marine Artificial Reef Development — A philosophical Review of Management". *Gulf of Mexico Science* 16, no. 1 (1998).
- Crutzen, P. "Geology of Mankind," *Nature* 415 (2002).
- National Oceanic and Atmospheric Association. "Ocean Pollution" http://www.noaa.gov/resource-collections/ocean- pollution. (accessed Jan 12, 2017).
- Wilkenson, B. "Humans as Geologic Agents: A Deep-time Perspective," *Geology* 33, no. 3 (2003).

THE HAMMAM OF ERBIL CITADEL

Project Name_ Hammam of Erbil; Location_ Erbil, Iraq

Image Credits_ Figure 01 – 04_ courtesy of the authors

BIBLIOGRAPHY:

- Al-Haidari, A. *Urban renewal for Erbil Citadel: tafseer office Erbil* (2014).
- Al-Haidari, A. *Popular bathrooms in Erbil between past and present:* Modern Discussion (2014).
- Al Yaqoobi, D. *Highlights of Erbil Citadel*. Erbil: Government Governorate of Erbil High commission of Erbil Citadel Revitalization (2012).
- Ahmed, A. *Hammam – Herbestemming als brug naar de toekomst van Erbil:* Universiteit Hasselt (2014). not published.
- Derbandi, N. A. *Hammam as a Koerdish heritage*. Subartu: Issued

by Kurdistan archaeologists syndicate. Second year, no. 2 (2008): 140 – 141.
- MacGinnis, J. *Erbil in the Cuneiform sources*. Erbil: Ministry of Culture and Youth, Kurdistan Regional Government (2013).
- Musatafa, M. J. *Art of Decoration and Ornaments on the Stone in Erbil:* University of Salahaddin-Erbil in partial fulfillment of the requirements for the degree of M.A.in Islamic Archaeology, 2011.
- Plevoets, B. & K. Van Cleempoel. "Adaptive reuse as an emerging discipline: an historic survey," In *Reinventing architecture and interiors: a socio-political view on building adaptation,* ed. G. Cairns, 13 – 32. London: Libri Publishers, 2013.
- Resul, E. *Erbil, a historical study of Erbil's intellectual and political Role.* Cultural Centre of the Ministry of Culture — the Kurdistan Regional Government publications (2005).
- Yaraly, B. *So do not forget Arbil:* tafseer office of publishing & advertising / Erbil (2001).

(re)MADE BY WATER

Project Name_ New World Mall, Bangkok, Thailand

Image Credits_ All images courtesy of the author; Figure 01_ Mall; central court, Photograph by Perfect Lazybones; Figure 02_ Floating market in Bangkok, Photograph by Georgie Pauwels: Figure 03_ Mall, escalators, Photograph by Olga Saliy: Figure 04_ Mall, koi, Photograph by Olga Saliy; Figure 05_ Mall, escalators, Photograph by Olga Saliy.

BIBLIOGRAPHY:

- Behnke, A. *Angkor Wat.* Minneapolis: Twenty-First Century Books, 2008.
- Benjamin, W. and M. Jennings. *The Writer of Modern Life: Essays on Charles Baudelaire.* Cambridge, MA: Belknap Press, 2006.
- Bharne, V. *The Emerging Asian City.* London: Routledge, 2013.
- Bharne, V. and K. Krusche. *Rediscovering the Hindu Temple: The Sacred Architecture and Urbanism of India.* Newcastle-upon-Tyne: Cambridge Scholars Publishing, 2012.
- Budziak, A. *Text, Body and Indeterminacy: The Doppelganger Selves in Pater and Wilde*. Newcastle-upon-Tyne: Cambridge Scholars, 2008.
- Burke, P. *The New Cambridge Modern History: Volume 13*. Cambridge: Cambridge University Press, 1979.
- Byrnes, Mark. "Removing Fish from a Surreal Abandoned Shopping Mall," *The Atlantic*, January 16, 2015.
- Foucault, M., and Miskowiec, J. "Of Other Spaces." *Diacritics* 16, no. 1 (1986): 22 – 27.
- Fredrickson, Terry. "Bangkok's hidden fish pond," *Bangkok Post*, July 1, 2014.
- Goldstein, Sasha. "Abandoned Bangkok shopping mall Becomes incredible koi pond after years of neglect," *New York Daily News*, July 1, 2014.
- Grossman, N. *Chronicle of Thailand: Headline News Since 1946*. Paris: Editions Didier Millet, 2009.
- Hadjiyanni, T. "Rethinking Culture in Interior Design Pedagogy: The Potential Beyond CIDA Standard 2g," *Journal of Interior Design* 38, no. 3 (2013).
- Heberle, L. and S. Opp. ed. *Local Sustainable Urban Development in a Globalized World.* London: Routledge, 2008.
- Hill, C. *South Asia: An Environmental History.* Santa Barbara: ABC-CLIO Publishing, 2008.
- Kongarchapatara, B., and R. Shannon. "Transformations in Thailand's Retailing Landscape: Public Policies, Regulations, and Strategies" in *Retailing in Emerging Markets: A Policy and Strategy Perspective*, ed. Malobi Mukherjee, Richard Cuthbertson, Elizabeth Howard. New York: Routledge.
- Lefebvre, H. *Critique of Everyday Life, Volume II.* Brooklyn: Verso, 2002.
- Leslie, E. "Ruin and Rubble in the Arcades," in *Walter Benjamin and the Arcades Project*, ed. Beatrice Hanssen. London: Bloomsbury, 2006.
- McDonough, T. *Guy Debord and the Situationist International: Texts and Documents*. Cambridge: The MIT Press, 2004.
- Peng, H. *Dandyism and Transcultural Modernity: The Dandy, the Flaneur, and the Translator in 1930s Shanghai, Tokyo, and Paris*. London: Routledge, 2015.
- Pleasance, Chris. "Splashing out at the shops: Hundreds of fish take over abandoned Thai mall after it's Flooded." *Daily Mail*, June 26, 2014.
- Sobocinska, A. "The Expedition's Afterlives: Echoes of Empire in Travel to Asia." In *Expedition into Empire: Exploratory Journeys and the Making of the Modern World*, ed. Martin Thomas. New York: Routledge, 2015.
- Turnbull, D. "Soc. Culture: Singapore." In *The Architecture of Fear,* ed. Nan Ellin. New York: Princeton Architectural Press, 1997.
- Vidler, A. *The Architectural Uncanny: Essays in the Modern Unhomely.* Cambridge: The MIT Press, 1994.
- Wancharoen, Supoj. "Fish pulled from New World pond." *Bangkok Post*, January 13, 2015.
- Wancharoen, Supoj. "A New World fish pond." *Bangkok Post*, June 30, 2014.

T-HOUSE

Project Name_ T-HOUSE, theoretical project; Location_ Hains Point, Washington, D.C.

Image Credits_ Figure 01 – 08_ courtesy of the authors

BIBLIOGRAPHY:

- Bell, Catherine. *Ritual: Perspectives and Dimensions*. New York: Oxford University Press, 1997.
- DeFerrari, John. "The Vanished Teahouse at Hains Point." Paper presented at the 40th Annual Conference on DC Historical Structures, Washington, D.C., November 14 – 17, 2013.
- "EPA, D.C. Area Students Officially Launch World Water Monitoring Day 2008." *US Newswire*, Alexandria, Virginia: September 18, 2008. Ga|A185264601.
- Howes, F.N. "Tea." Review of *Tea* by T. Eden. *Nature* 4649 (1958): 1577.
- Jackson, J.R. "Tea." *Nature*, July 14, 1870: 215 – 217.
- James, H. *The Portrait of a Lady*. New York: Random House, the Modern Library, 1851.
- Okakura, K. *The Book of Tea*. Rutland, Vermont: Charles E. Tuttle Company, 1956.
- Proust, M. *Swann's Way.* Translated by Lydia Davis. New York: Penguin Books, 2003.
- Sen, H. Afterword to *The Book of Tea,* by Kakuzo Okakura. Translated by the Urasenke Foundation, Foreign Affairs Division. Tokyo: Kodansha International, Ltd., 1989.
- Tafuri, M. *The Sphere and the Labyrinth: Avant-Gardes and Architecture from Piranesi to the 1970s*. Cambridge: The MIT Press, 1992.
- Thomas, F. "Tea." *New England Review* 33, no. 1 (2012): 82 – 87.
- Wedzicha, B.L. "Tea." *Nutrition & Food Science* 79, iss. 6 (1979): 2 – 4.

THE BLUE LINE

Project Name_ blue developments; Location_ Battir, Palestine; Qeparo, Albania

Image Credits_ Figure 01- illustration by author

BIBLIOGRAPHY:
- De Sherbinin, A.; A. Schiller.; A. Pulsipher. "The vulnerability of global cities to climate hazards." *Environ. Urban.* 19 (2007): 26 – 39.
- Farmer, B. H. "Perspectives on the 'Green Revolution' in South Asia." *Modern Asian Studies* 20, no. 1 (1986): 175 – 199.
- McDonald, R.I.; P. Green; D. Balk.; B.M. Fekete.; C. Revenga; M. Todd; M. Montgomery. "Urban growth, climate change, and freshwater availability." *Proc. Natl. Acad. Sci. USA* 108 (2011): 6312 – 6317.
- Schuetze, T.; L. Chelleri. "Integrating Decentralized Rainwater Management in Urban Planning and Design: Flood Resilient and Sustainable Water Management Using the Example of Coastal Cities in The Netherlands and Taiwan". *Water* 5 (2013): 593 – 616.
- Shiklomnov, I. "World fresh water resources" in *Water in Crisis: a guide to the World's Fresh Water Resources.* edited by Gleick P.H. New York: Oxford University Press.
- UN, "International decade for action 'Water for life' 2005 – 2015." http://www.un.org/waterforlifedecade/scarcity.shtml (accessed November 6th, 2016).
- World DataBank, World Bank. "Rural population (% of total population)." http://data.worldbank.org/indicator/SP.RUR.TOTL.ZS (accessed November 6th, 2016).

ENVIRONMENTAL IDENTITY

Project Name 01_ Caiaques kayaks; Location_ Pinheiros River, São Paulo, Brazil; Artist_ Eduardo Srur; Project Name 02_Pets; Location_ Tietê River in São Paulo, Brazil; Artist_ Eduardo Srur

Image Credits_ All photos courtesy of Eduardo Srur; Figure 01_ Caiaques, kayaks, Pinheiros River, photo_ Eduardo Nicolau; Figure 02_ Caiaques, kayaks, Pinheiros River, photo_Alexandre Schneider; Figure 03_ Pets, Tietê River, photo_Eduardo Srur; Figure 04_ Pets, Tietê River, photo_ Almeida Rocha

BIBLIOGRAPHY:
- Brocaneli, Pérola Felipette. *O ressurgimento das águas na paisagem paulistana: fator fundamental para a cidade sustentável.* Phd diss., Universidade de Sao Paulo, 2007
- Carvalho, Fabíola Araújo de. *Caminho das águas: A água na cidade de São Paulo.* Sao Paulo, Revista Belas Artes 13 (2013): 1 – 43, url http://www.belasartes.br/revistabelasartes/?pagina=player&slug=caminho-das-aguas-a-agua-na-cidade-de-sao-paulo (accessed February 25, 2017)

A METROPOLITAN PARK OF WATER

Project Name_ Metropolitan Water Park project, Location_ Saragossa, Spain

Image Credits_ Figure 01_ Bridge Pavilion & Third Millennium Bridge, Río Ebro, Zaragoza, España, Source_Pabellón Puente y Puente del Tercer Milenio, Author_ Juan E De Cristofaro from Zaragoza, España, CC-BY-SA-2.0; Figure 02_Google Earth aerial view of Zaragoza, Spain; Figure 03_ Plano topográfico de la ciudad de Zaragoza del siglo XVIII, Wikimedia;

BIBLIOGRAPHY:
- Ebropolis, *Plan Estratégico de Zaragoza y su entorno*, Zaragoza 2006.
- Ezquiaga, J.M., "El lugar: Zaragoza y la Expo", *Arquitectura viva* 117, *Pabellón de Espana Expo Zaragoza 2008*, (2007).
- La Expo de Zaragoza acumula unas pérdidas de 502 millones de euros, *El Periódico de Aragón*, April 04, 2010.
- Lecardane, R., G. Cimadomo. "Las grandes exposiciones en Europa1992 – 2002. Efectos duraderos sobre la ciudad y apropriación por parte de la ciudadanía", in *Proceedings of International Seminar on World Events and Urban Change, Grupo de Investigación HUM-700*, Siviglia, 2012.
- Lecardane, R., "Expo, ville, architecture. Lisbonne et l'héritage de l'Expo'98, in *Cahiers thématiques — L'architecture et l'événement*, 8 (2009), 127 – 135.
- Martínez Ramírez, I.M., "Las estaciones del ferrocarril Zaragoza-Caminreal, vistas por sus autores, los arquitectos Luis Gutiérrez Soto y Secundino Zuazo Ugalde." *Artigrama* 14 (1999): 99 – 107.

BETWEEN RESILIENCY AND ADAPTATION

Image Credits_ All images courtesy of the author; Figure 01_ by author, background_ by Aleks Dahlberg at www.unsplash.com; Figure 02_ by author; Figure 03, 04_ graphic by author, background_ by Frantzou Fleurine; www.unsplash.com

BIBLIOGRAPHY:
- Buchanan, L., H. Fairfield, A. Parlapiano, S. Peçanha, T. Wallace, D. Watkins and K. Yourish.
- Erickson, C. "Crumple Zones in Automobiles," *Sourced through the American Institute of Physics*. (accessed July 28. 2015).
- Guattari, F. *The Three Ecologies*. 1989, Trans. Ian Pindar and Paul Sutton. New Brunswick, NJ: Athlone P, 2000.
- "Mapping the Destruction of Typhoon Haiyan", *The New York Times*. November 11, 2013. http://www.nytimes.com/interactive/2013/11/11/world/asia/typhoon-haiyan-map.html
- NOAA. "Storm Surge Overview", *National Hurricane Center | National Oceanic and Atmospheric Administration*. http://www.nhc.noaa.gov/surge/. August 27, 2015.
- Reed, C., and N. Lister. "Parallel Genealogie." In *Projective ecologies*. New York, 2014.
- Schwartz, J. "How to Save a Sinking Coast? Katrina Created a Laboratory", *The New York Times | Science*. August 7, 2015. http://www.nytimes.com/2015/08/08/science/louisiana-10-years-after-hurricane-katrina.html?_r=0
- Wu, J., and W. Tong. "Ecological resilience as a foundation for urban design and sustainability", In *Resilience in Ecology and Urban Design* 3 (2013): 211 – 229.

WATER AS MEDIUM

Project Name 01_ Water tower in Delft, Architect_ Rocha Tombal; Location_ Delft, NL; Project name 02_ Water tower in Brasschaat, Architect_ Crepain-Binst Architects; Location_ Brasschaat, Belgium; Project name 3_ Water tower Sint-Jans convent, Overijssel; Architect_ Zecc Architects; Location_ Overijssel, NL

Image Credits_All images courtesy of the authors_ Figure 01_ typological evolution of the water tower, Source: Inge Donné; Figure 02_ Water tower in Delft (NL), photo by Christiaan Richters; Figure 03, 04, 05_ Water tower in Brasschaat (BE), Crepain-Binst Architects, photo_ Crepain Binst; Figure 06, 07_ Water tower Sint-Jans convent, Overijssel (NL), Zecc Architects, photo_ Stijn Poelstra, http://www.stijnstijl.nl/;

BIBLIOGRAPHY:
- Cercleux, A.-L., Mercliu F.-C., Peptenatu D. "Conversion of water towers — An instrument for conserving heritage assets." *Urbanism architectura constructi* 5, no. 2 (2014): 3 – 19.
- Norberg- Schulz, C. *Genius loci: Towards a phenomenology of architecture*. New York: Rizzoli, 1980.
- Van Craenenbroeck, W. *Eenheid in verscheidenheid watertorens in Belgie.* Brussels: NAVEWA, 1991.

COLOPHON

Ahmed Abbas holds a Bachelor Degree in Architecture from the Technical University of Avans and a Master in Interior Architecture from Hasselt University in Belgium. He has six years of experience as an architect in leading his own company. He has been a lecturer at the University of Newroz (Iraq) since 2014, where he teaches Modern Design and coordinates Working / Drawing and Building Construction. Since 2015 he has been working on his Ph.D. entitled "A Proposed Methodology for the Adaptive Reuse of Traditional Buildings in the Buffer Zone of Erbil Citadel".

Brian Ambroziak is an Associate Professor of Architecture at the University of Tennessee, Knoxville. His publications include *Michael Graves: Images of a Grand Tour* (2005) and *Infinite Perspectives: Two Thousand Years of Three Dimensional Mapmaking* (1999) with Princeton Architectural Press. In 2008, Brian Ambroziak founded time[scape]lab with Andrew McLellan and Katherine Ambroziak.

Katherine Bambrick Ambroziak is an Associate Professor of Architecture at the University of Tennessee, Knoxville. Her publications include *DeadSpace Arlington*, *Material Scribe: Memoirs of the Collective Individual*, *Surrogate Stones*, *Odd Fellows: Constructing the Positive Place|Self*, and *Codification of Ritual in Design*. Since 2009, she has served as the primary designer and coordinator of the Odd Fellows Cemetery Reclamation Project, a conservation and rehabilitation initiative that aims to educate and support the minority communities of East Knoxville through the design and implementation of a responsive memorial landscape.

Michael Leighton Beaman is the founding principal of Beta-field, a design/research office run with Landscape Architect and educator Zaneta Hong. Michael is also a co-founding member of the design nonprofit GA Collaborative. Michael currently teaches at the University of Virginia where he is an Assistant Professor in Architecture and at the Rhode Island School of Design, where he is a critic in the Interior Architecture Dept. In addition to teaching and practice, Michael is a writer for *Architectural Record* focusing on design technologies and techno-centric design practices.

Inge Donné completed her bachelor's degree in Interior Architecture at Lucca School of Arts, Brussels, and her master's degree on the topic of adaptive reuse at Hasselt University. After internships at Baccarne and Lens°ass architects, she researched the reuse of water towers and created a masterproject for the water tower of Hoeilaart (BE) as co-working space.

Dr Graeme Evans is Professor of Urban Design at Middlesex University, Department of Design and Director of the Art & Design Research Institute. He has been leading a research project in the Lee Valley as part of a 3 year Arts & Humanities Research Council-funded project: Towards Hydrocitizenship, exploring the changing relationships between people, ecosystems and urban water landscapes, and the legacy of waterside architecture and heritage. In June 2015 he curated the Hackney Wick & Fish Island Connecting Communities Festival including an exhibition of site-based design schemes including BA Interior Architecture student work, as part of the London Festival of Architecture. Graeme is also Professor of Culture & Urban Development at Maastricht University, The Netherlands where he has been working on several industrial heritage re-use schemes.

Alexander Ford earned a B.S. in Architecture from the University of Arizona in 2014, and an M.S. in Historic Preservation from Columbia University in 2016. Ford currently works for Daniel Libeskind in New York. His architectural work has been published internationally.

Francesco Garofalo founded Openfabric in 2011, an office specialized in landscape architecture and urban planning based in the Netherlands. Francesco Garofalo studied Landscape Architecture in Van Hall Larenstein Arnhem, the Netherlands and in Genoa University. Through Openfabric he has led various awarded competitions and commissions, including: a proposal for New Tahrir square in Cairo, Egypt; an AIDS memorial park, New York, USA; renewal of the main boulevard in Genoa — Via XX Settembre, Italy (First prize); an urban square, realized in The Hague, The Netherlands (First prize). Francesco currently teaches at the Amsterdam Academy.

Nicholas Gervasi earned a B.ARCH and M.ARCH from Tulane University in 2012, and an M.S. in Historic Preservation from Columbia University in 2016. Gervasi currently works for AYON Studio Architecture and Preservation in New York.

Naomi House is a Designer, Educator and Writer with an approach to the Interior that is framed through forensic investigation. A Senior Lecturer in Interior Architecture at Middlesex University she is also a Tutor in Critical and Historical Studies at the Royal College of Art. Naomi is a founding member and Superintendent of C.I.D — the *Council of Inordinate Design*.

Catherine R Joseph is an architect based in New York City. She earned a Master of Architecture from Cornell University and a Bachelor of Science in Structural Engineering from Duke University.

Paola La Scala PLS, architect, she is *Doctor Europaeus in Museography* (Palermo). In 2013 attended, as a guest PhD student, the School of Museum Studies at University of Leicester (UK). Since 2013 she has been taking an active part in L@bCity Architecture, a research group headed by Prof. Renzo Lecardane at Department of Architecture in Palermo, concerning architecture and city planning, focusing on culture as important strategy for urban regeneration. Currently she is working on the use of digital technologies to enhance architectural heritage.

Renzo Lecardane, Ph.D. in Architectural Design (Palermo) and *docteur de l'Ecole Nationale des Ponts et Chaussées* (Paris), is Associate Professor in Architectural Design at Department of Architecture of University of Palermo. From 2000 to 2005 he carried out research and teaching activities in France (EAPMalaquais, EAPLa Villette, EAPVal de Seine; LATTS/ENPC-Paris; GRAI). From 2002 is associate to *Laboratoire Infrastructure, Architecture, Territoire* (ENSAPMalaquais). Since 2009 he is member of the Academic Board for the PhD in Architecture at University of Palermo. In 2013 he founded the research group *L@bCity Architecture* creating connections between architectural design and urban shape.

Karen Lens holds a Master in Architecture and Architecture Sciences from Sint-Lucas and KU Leuven, both in Belgium. She worked for 10 years as an architect specializing in adaptive reuse, energy efficiency and design for all. In 2012, Karen started a Ph.D. on the reinterpretation of underused monastic sites in Limburg (Belgium) and Western Europe at Hasselt University. She is also engaged in several design studios concerning adaptive reuse and collective dwelling at the same university.

Kees Lokman is an Assistant Professor of Landscape Architecture at the University of British Columbia. He holds degrees in planning, urban design and landscape architecture. Current research focusing on the intersection of landscape, infrastructure and ecology has been published in the Journal of Architectural Education, Topos, Landscapes|Paysages and New Geographies. Kees is also founder of Parallax Landscape, a collaborative and interdisciplinary design and research platform. klokman@sala.ubc.ca www.parallaxlandscape.com

Gregory Marinic an associate professor and head of the environmental and interior design program in the Syracuse University School of Design. His research and practice are focused on the intersection of architecture, interiors, obsolescence, geography, and adaptive reuse. A widely published design scholar and researcher, Marinic has served as an editor/associate editor of several international peer-reviewed publications, and as co-founder of the *International Journal of Interior Architecture & Design*. His most recent publications include *Journal of Architectural Education*, *Journal of Interior Design*, *AD Journal*, *Design Issues*, *International Journal of Architectural Research*, *IntAR Journal of Interventions and Adaptive Reuse*, and various publications of the Association of Collegiate Schools of Architecture.

Bie Plevoets studied Interior Architecture at the PHL University College in Hasselt (BE) and Conservation of Monuments and Sites at the Raymond Lemaire International Centre for Conservation in Leuven (BE). In 2014, she obtained a PhD in architecture at Hasselt University; her thesis was entitled 'retail-reuse: an interior view on adaptive reuse of buildings'. Her current research focuses on the theory of adaptive reuse, and preservation of spirit of place. She teaches courses on adaptive reuse at Hasselt University in the specialized master programme in Interiors 'Adaptive Reuse — exploring spatial potentials and the poetics of the existing'.

Anne Schraiber is a practicing architect based in São Paulo, Brazil. She holds a bachelor degree in Architecture and Urban Planning from Universidade Mackenzie (2006) and a Master in Business Administration from Fundação Armando Álvares Penteado (2010). She continued her education at a postgraduate course in Ephemeral Architecture at Escuela Técnica Superior de Arquitectura de Madrid (2015). Anne was a participant at the 10th São Paulo Architecture Biennale (2013) and won a best interior design project award at CASACOR TRIO (2011). Her academic interest focus on the research of the ephemeral design in the contemporary culture.

Lindsay Winstead is an architectural designer working in San Francisco, California for Rapt Studio. She began her career at Davis Brody Bond in New York City, after which she received a Masters of Design in Adaptive Reuse, from the Rhode Island School of Design. Some of her built work includes the US Embassy Compound in Jakarta, Indonesia, Vivint Solar's headquarters in Lehi, Utah, and Lydian Dental in Tempe, Arizona.

EDITORS

Ernesto Aparicio is a Senior Critic in the Department of Graphic Design at RISD. Aparicio earned his BA at the Escuela de Bellas Artes, La Plata, Buenos Aires and completed his Post Graduate Studies at the Ecole des Art Decoratifs, Paris. Prior to moving to the US, he served as Art Director for Editions du Seuil in Paris, while maintaining his own graphic design practice, Aparicio Design Inc. Best known for his work in the world of publishing, Aparicio has worked on corporate identities, publications, and way-finding for corporations and institutions in France, Japan, and the US. Recently, Aparicio was named Creative Director for the New York firm DFA.

Markus Berger is Associate Professor and Graduate Program Director in the Department of Interior Architecture at RISD. Berger holds a Diplomingenieur für Architektur from the Technische Universität Wien, Austria and is a registered architect (SBA) in the Netherlands. Prior to coming to the US, Berger practiced and taught in the Netherlands, Austria, India, and Pakistan, and currently heads his own art and design studio in Providence. His work, research, writing, and teaching focus on art and design interventions in the built environment, including issues of historic preservation, sensory experience and alteration. He is a co-founder and co-editor of the Int|AR Journal.

Liliane Wong is Professor and Head of the Department of Interior Architecture at RISD. Wong received her Masters of Architecture from Harvard University, Graduate School of Design and a Bachelor of Art in Mathematics from Vassar College. She is a registered Architect in Massachusetts and has practiced in the Boston area, including in her firm, MWA.She is the author of *Adaptive Reuse_Extending the Lives of Buildings*, co-author of *Libraries: A Design Manual* and contributing author of *Designing Interior Architecture and Flexible Composite Materials in Architecture, Construction and Interiors*. A long time volunteer at soup kitchens, she emphasizes the importance of public engagement in architecture and design in her teaching. Wong is a co-founder and co-editor of the Int|AR Journal.